CW01653243

DAVID TRESS

2015

MESSUM'S

www.messums.com

28 Cork Street, London W1S 3NG
Telephone: +44 (0)20 7437 5545

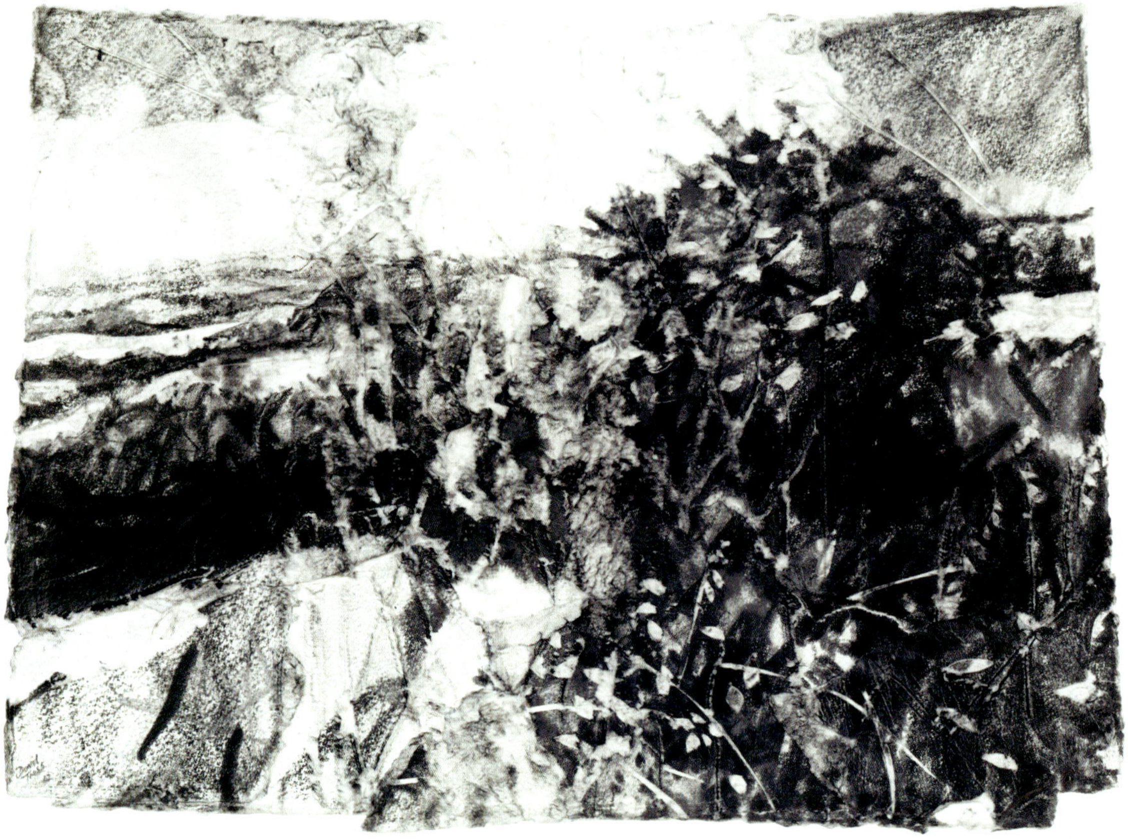

David Tress: 60 Not Out

An exhibition in honour of David Tress's 60th birthday is an occasion for celebration no less than an opportunity for retrospection and reassessment. With that in mind I have compiled a substantial monograph on the artist and his work, based on a friendship of more than 20 years' duration, and a lasting interest in his work. That book is published to coincide with the present exhibition and the significant birthday, but a catalogue focusing specifically on his latest work was also deemed appropriate: hence this short introduction.

These days, Tress principally makes mixed media paintings on paper, and drawings in graphite or charcoal. No longer does he work in oils on canvas, and the brilliance of his work has much to do with the white of the paper shining through his acrylics and other media. Among the drawings is the splendid graphite *Wet Day (St Martin's in the Fields)*, in which the grand Trafalgar Square church looks as if suddenly transported to Venice, and seen across a stretch of canal or sea. At the same time the image is marvellously evocative of

2 Uncertain Summer (Elderflower), 2012 graphite on paper 30 x 42 cms 11¾ x 16½ ins Pembrokeshire

3 Red Hill (Llanthony), 2012 mixed media on paper 65 x 84 cms 25⅝ x 33⅛ ins Monmouthshire

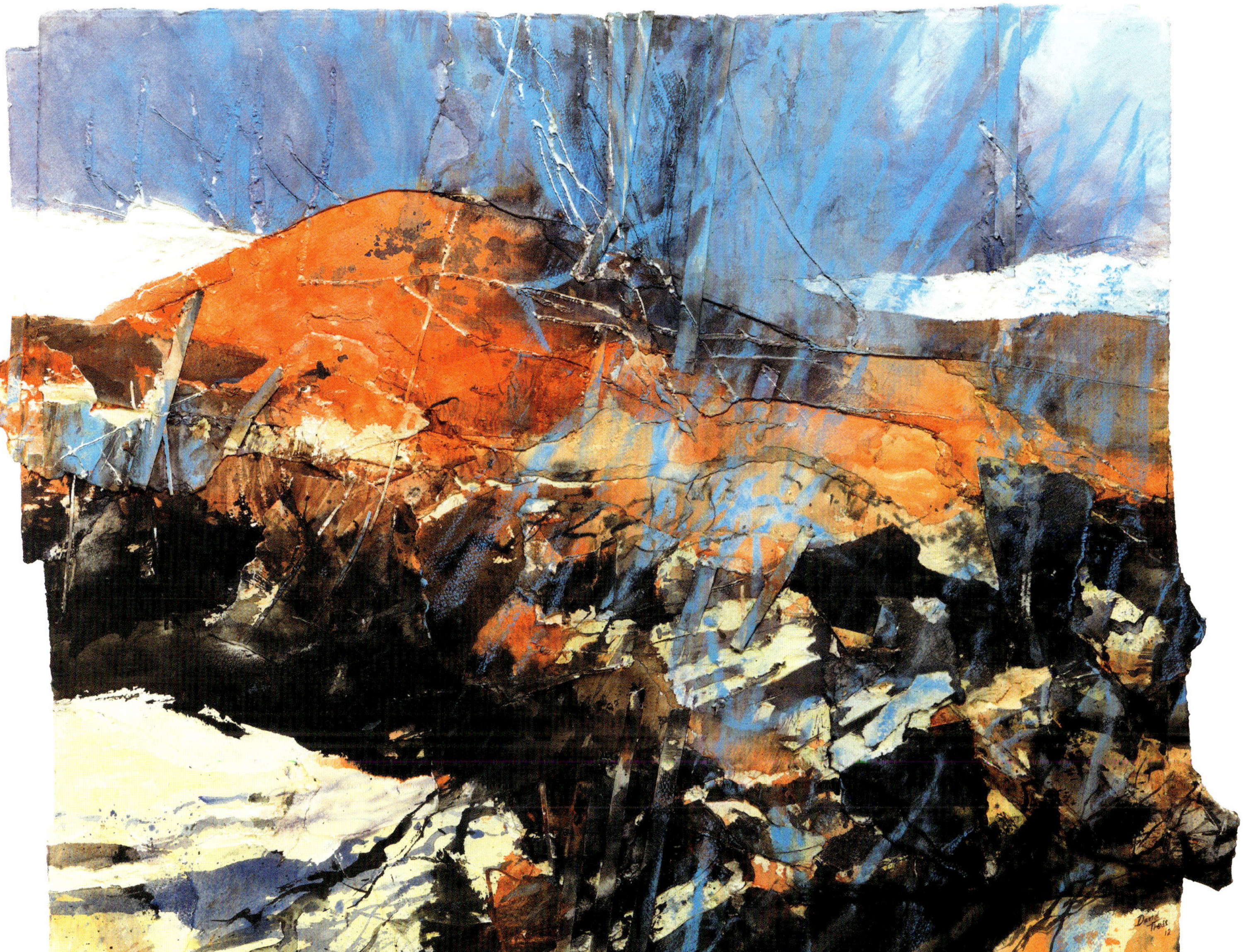

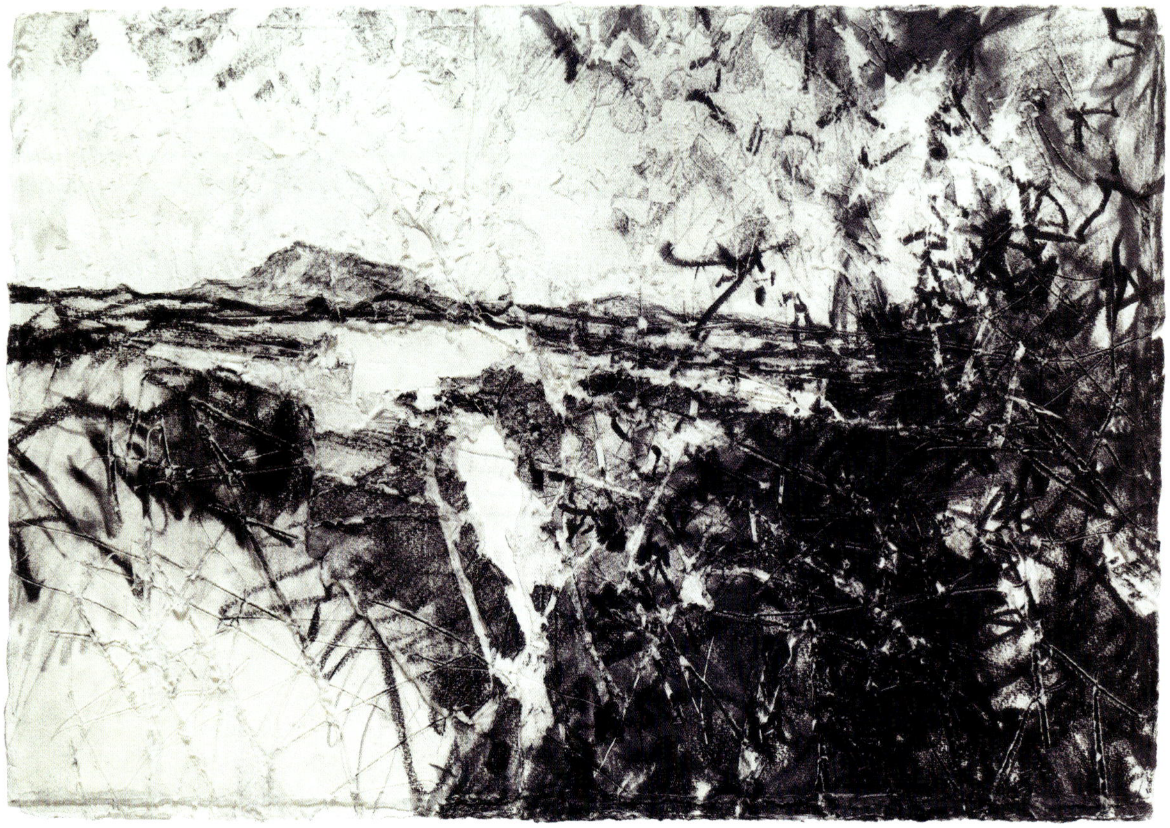

wet days in London and full of reflections. Notice the impact of the middle distance in a drawing like *The Land is Always. Carn Rhosson*, or the formal structure of *Rain in the Wind (Hayfields, Eskdale)*.

Tress plays off his lights and darks, his textures and surface patterns with great aplomb. He is a superbly skilful and atmospheric draughtsman, re-stating in every work his fundamental belief that you cannot be an artist without knowing the traditional disciplines of how to draw and paint. Although there may be shortcuts in current paintings (made possible by long experience and technical dexterity), there were none in his career, and he learnt the hard way, by trial and error and continual application. He worked through the established techniques of watercolour and oil painting to develop the mixed media on paper approach he favours now. He wouldn't be able to do what he does today without that history of dedication and struggle.

Tress engages with the numinous in nature, the spirit of place identified by Wordsworth in the

4 The Land Is Always. Carn Rhosson, 2011 graphite on paper 40 x 58 cms 15¾ x 22⅞ ins Pembrokeshire

5 Llanthony Valley, First Light, 2014 mixed media on paper 48 x 67 cms 18⅞ x 26⅜ ins Monmouthshire

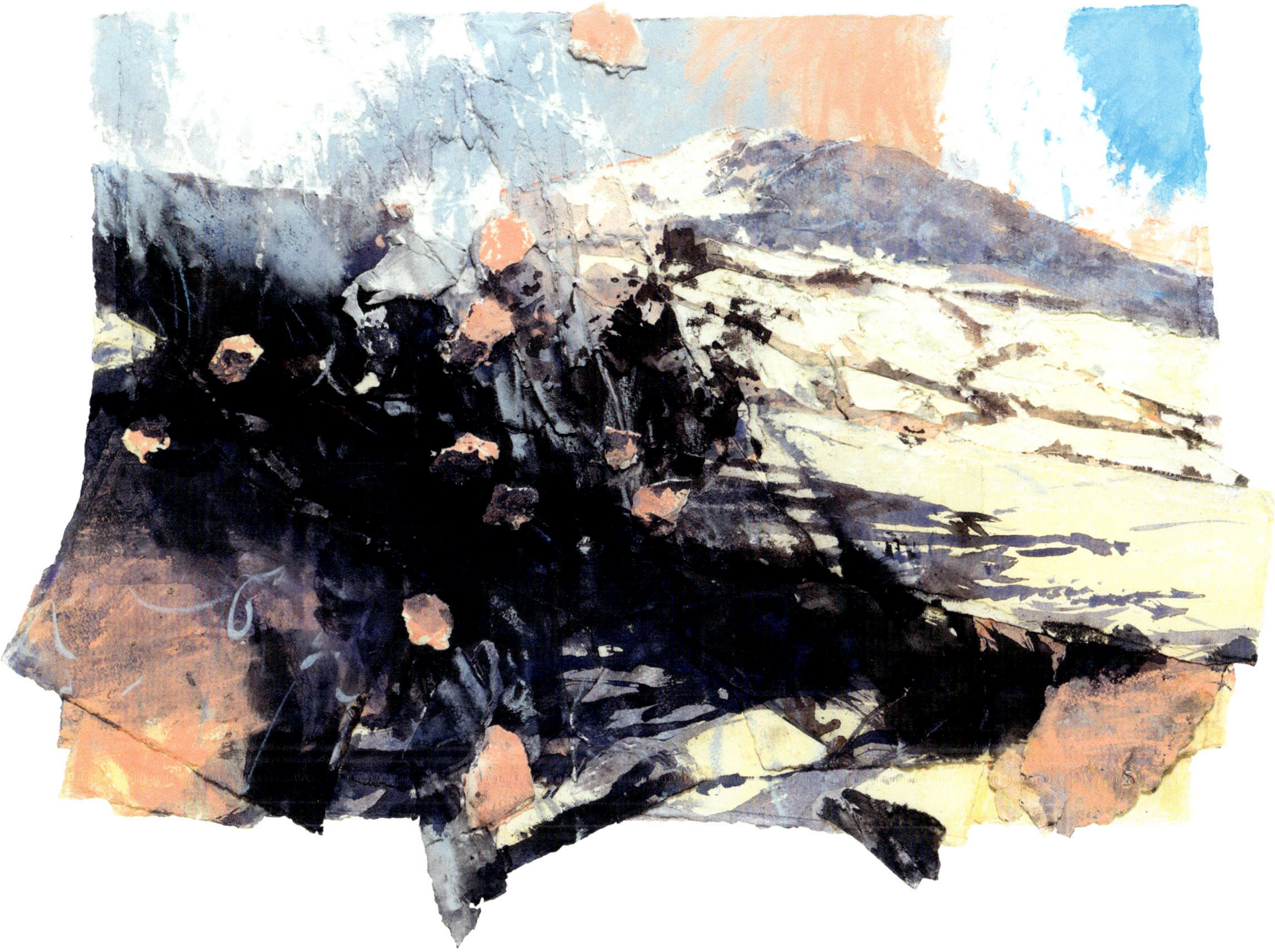

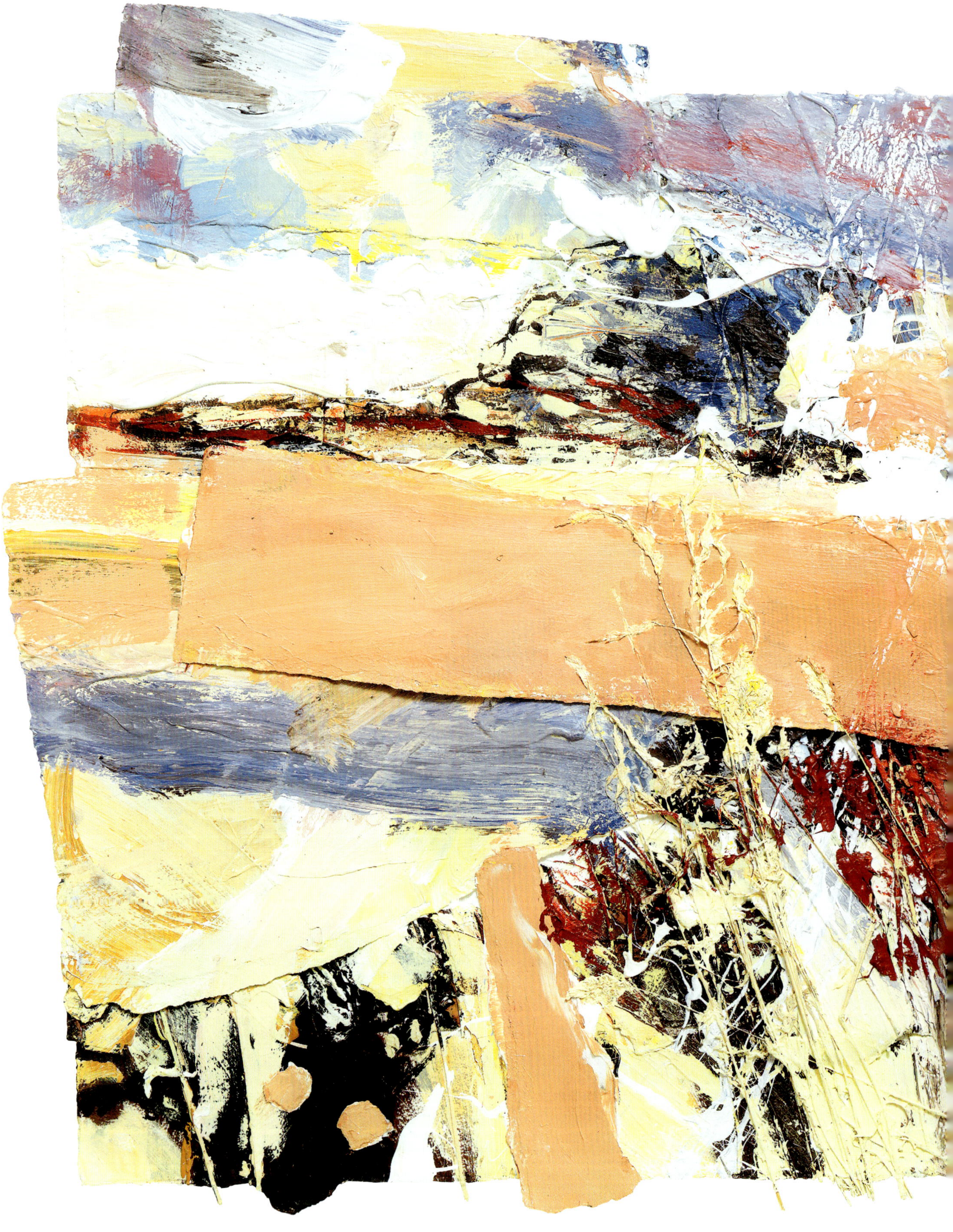

6 The Land (Winter, Pen Beri), 2014 mixed media on paper 91 x 151 cms 35⅞ x 59½ ins Pembrokeshire

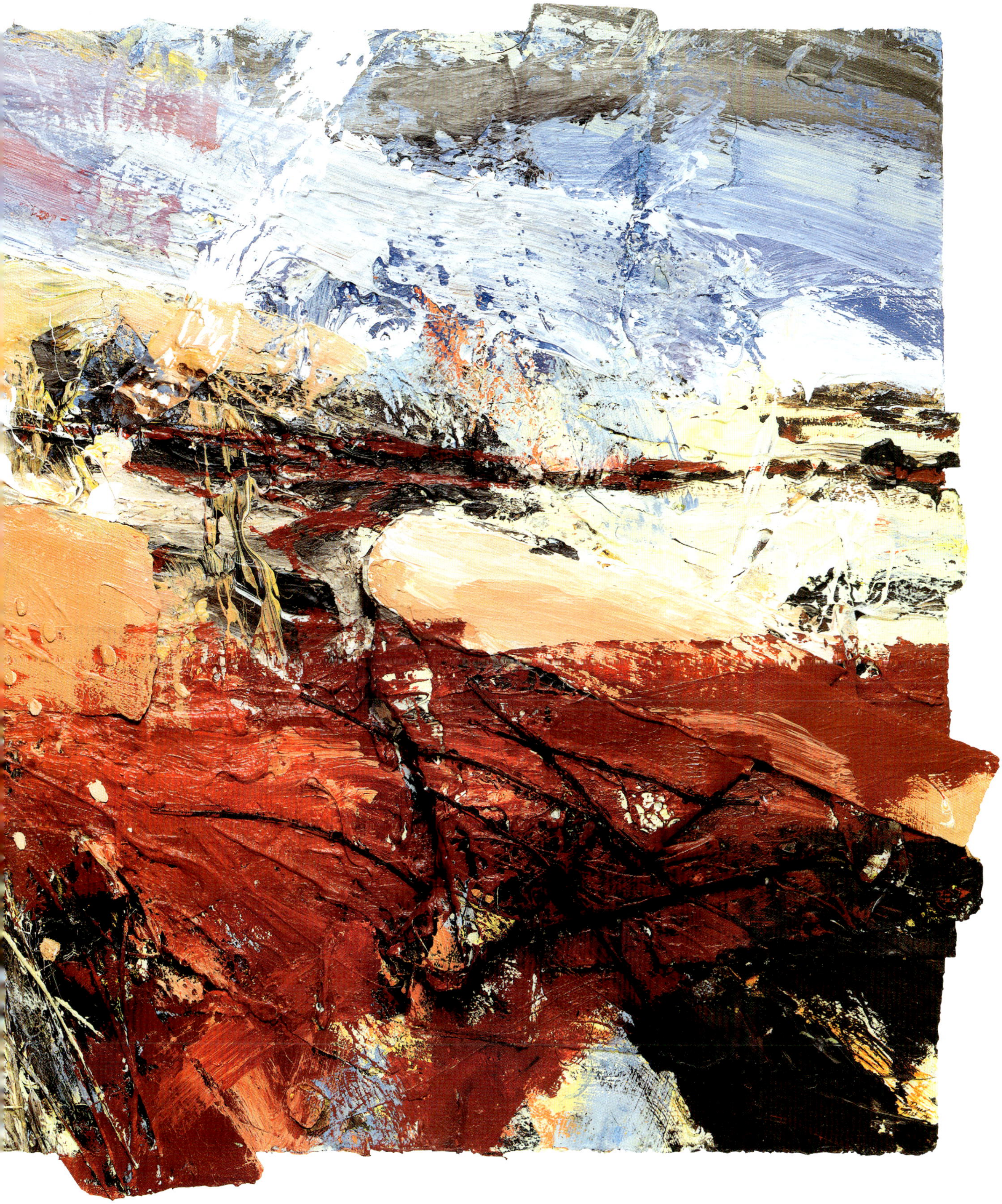

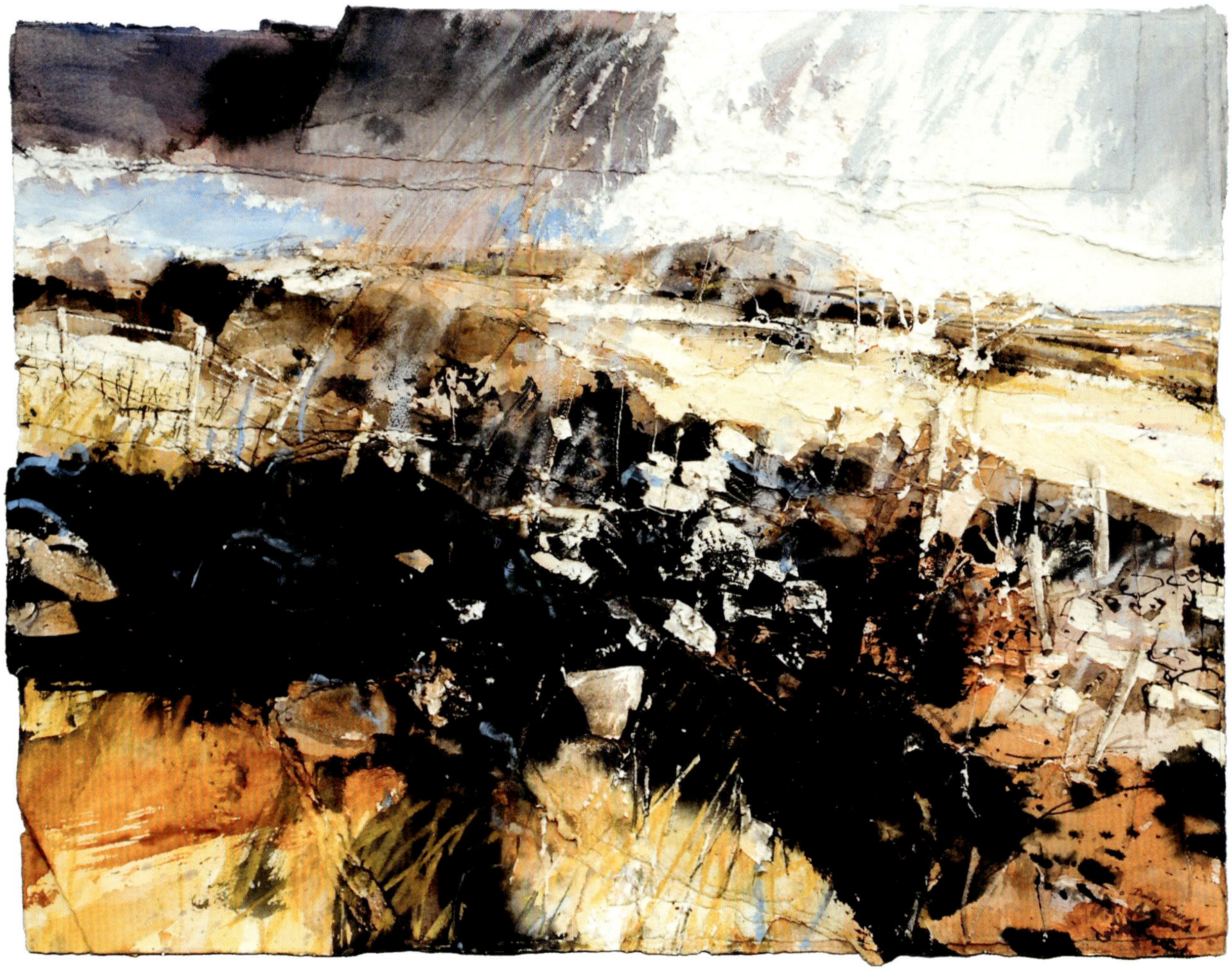

famous lines:

One impulse from a vernal wood
May teach you more of man
Of moral evil and of good
Than all the sages can

He tries to penetrate behind the obvious in landscape, to get beneath the picturesque postcard look and identify the significant. He loves Pembrokeshire where he lives because he recognizes there a real sense of the living presence of the past. His paintings investigate the archaeology of landscape through a dialogue between topography and abstraction – abstraction with an expressionist rather than geometric bias. Returning to the same places time and again, at different seasons (spring and autumn being his preferred times) over the passage of years, allows him to move away from topography towards an essential elemental expression. His metaphysical and formal approach is geared to finding the unexpected and voicing the unsaid. In the final analysis, the painting is always about landscape,

7 Year Ending (Pencaer), 2010 mixed media on paper 60 x 78 cms 23⅝ x 30¾ ins Pembrokeshire

8 I Can Feel It (Spring Coming, Carn Llidi), 2014 mixed media on paper 53 x 62 cms 20⅞ x 24⅜ ins Pembrokeshire

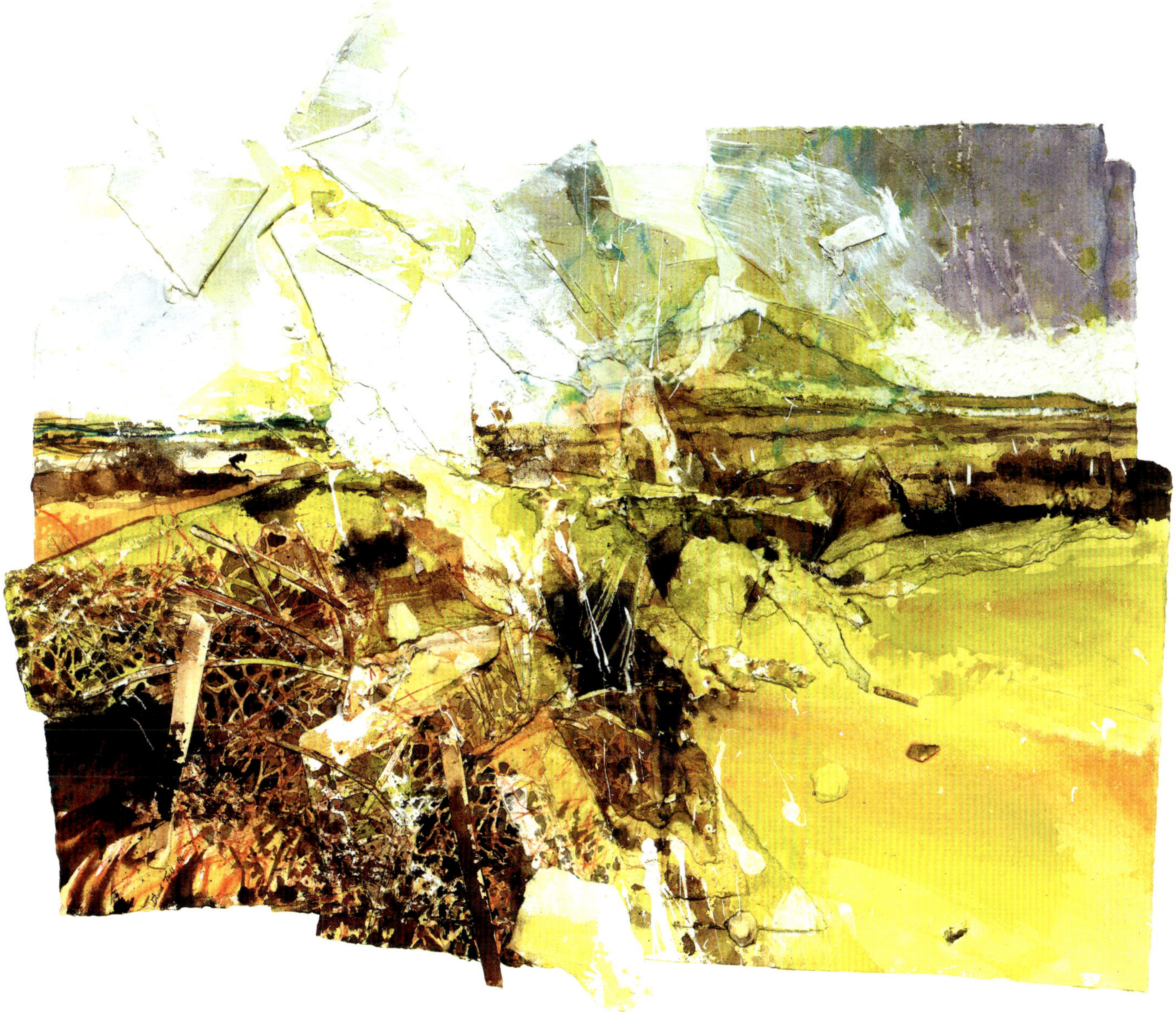

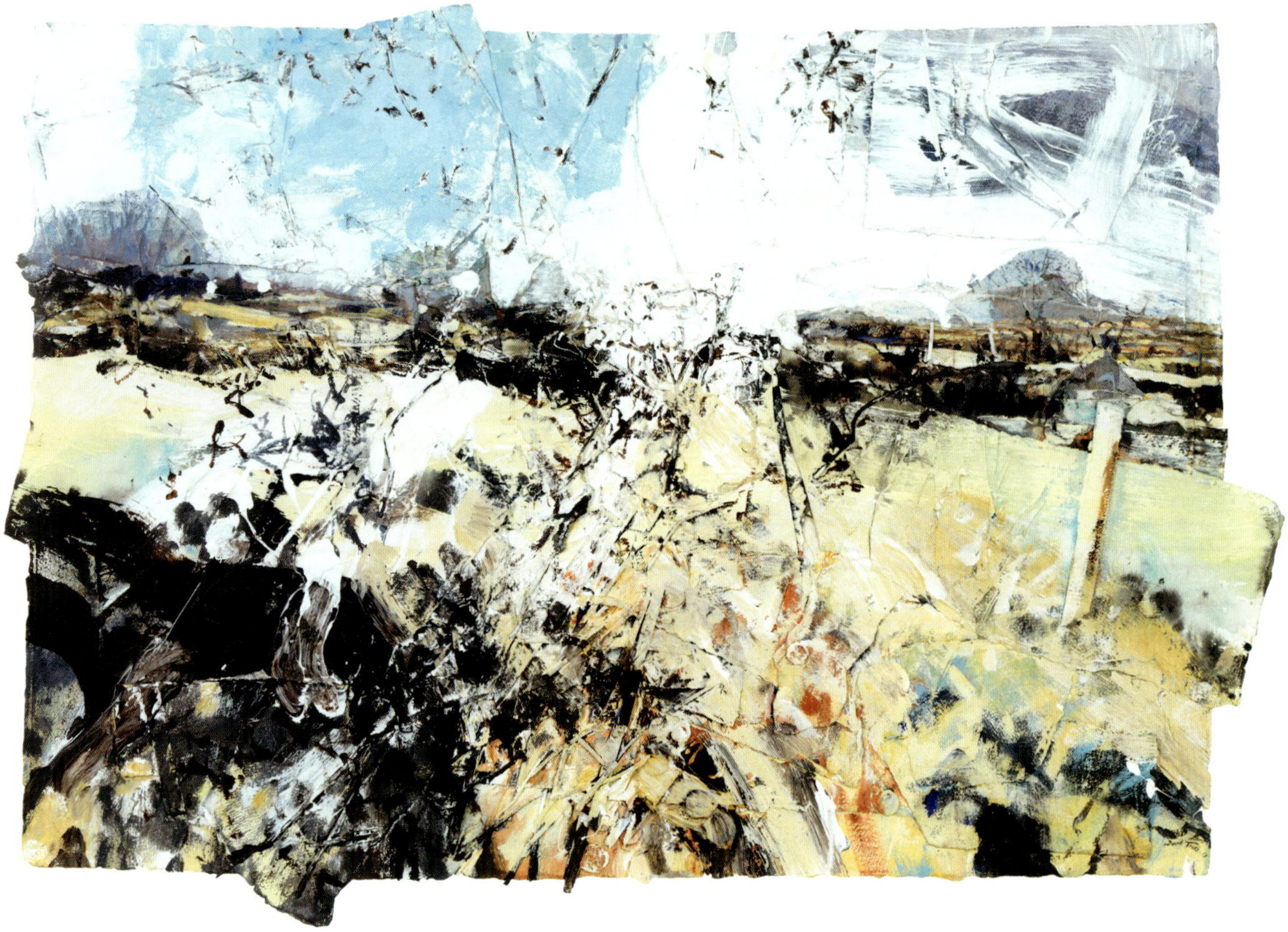

but it is also about the artist's visceral response to a place and its history. And it's about states of mind: a sense of ourselves in relation to the environment.

Tress's paintings stimulate the imagination through the sheer elation of looking. All the excitement and dynamism of his work is directed towards this end. This is why in the process of making he may attack and do violence to his materials: scoring, gouging and ripping the paper. He doesn't want to make polite pictures, he is in pursuit of something altogether more visionary. For him, violence of attack is a way of accessing elemental truths and producing, for instance, an equivalent statement to the act of erosion on soil and rock.

There are so many fine things here that all I can do is mention a few especial favourites. I love for instance, the Llanthony paintings, which seem to have a particularly broad sumptuousness and depth of colour. Against their rich reds the wonderful intensity of fresh leafage in *Green Spring Valley Bud Burst* detonates on the eye with riotous delight. *Turn Left for Muckish (Donegal)*, apart from

9 Looking (January), 2013 mixed media on paper 74 x 105 cms 29⅛ x 41⅜ ins Pembrokeshire

10 Wet Spring, 2014 mixed media on paper 62 x 81 cms 24⅜ x 31⅞ ins Pembrokeshire

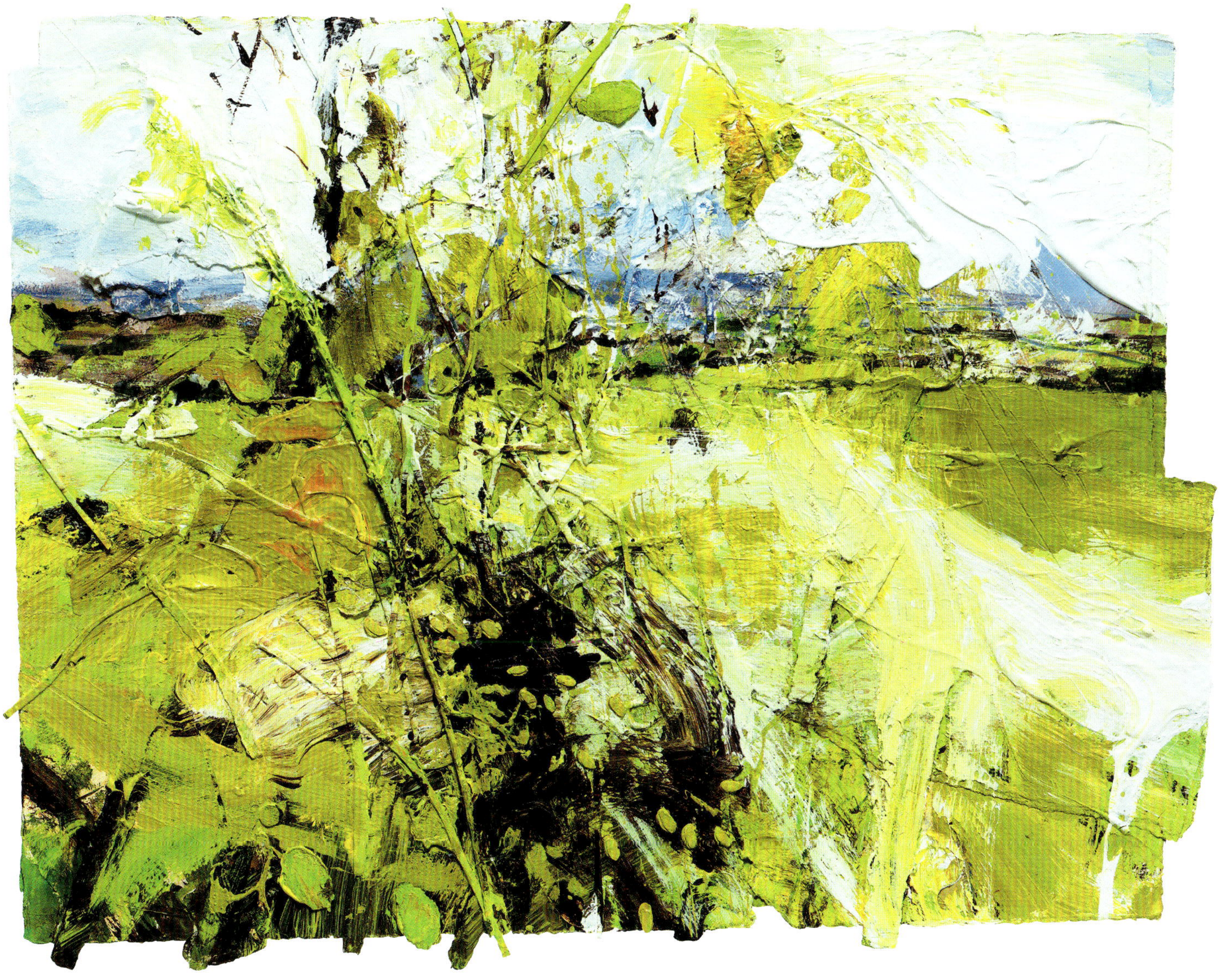

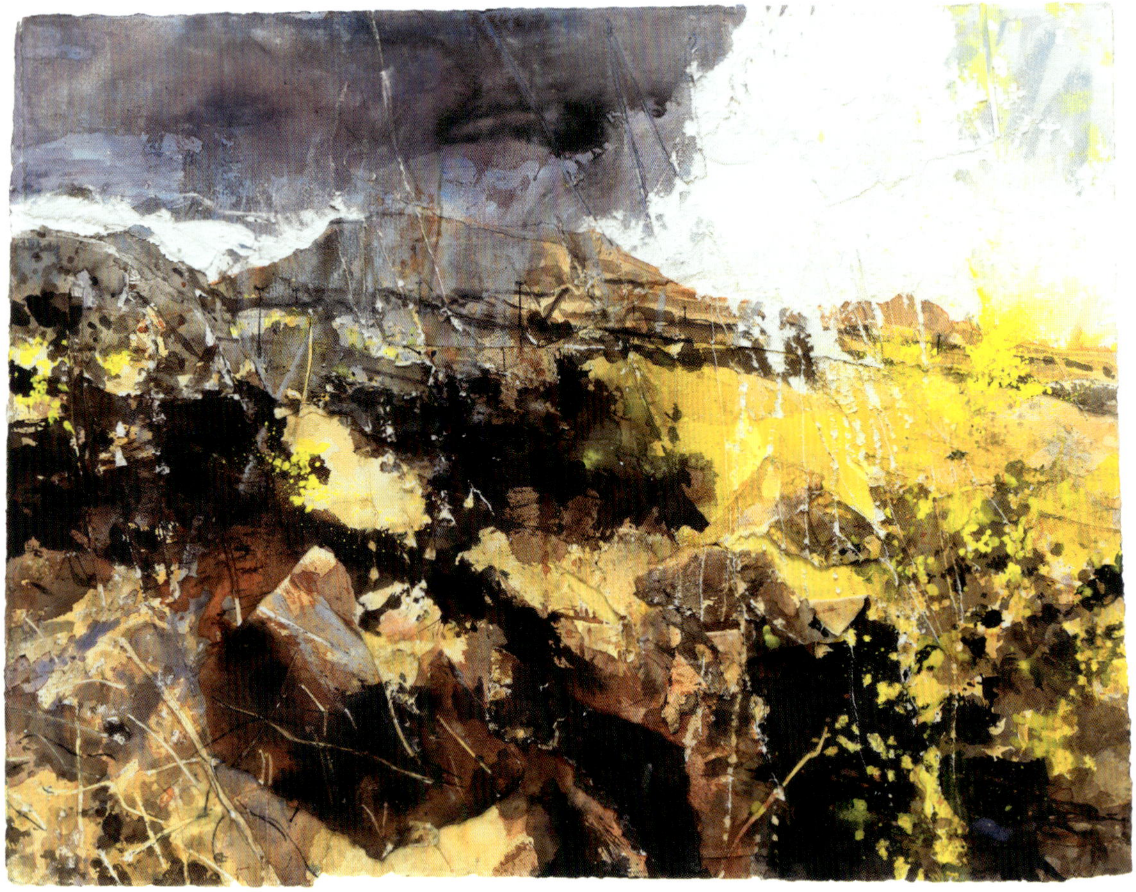

its beguiling title, is a fine example of Tress the employer of signs, with its potent black chevrons slashing across the picture space. Meanwhile two North Yorkshire church interiors focus on tub fonts dissolving in light. Tress says modestly that he has no specific religious belief, but in these paintings – and in so many of his others – he identifies the spiritual importance of place with gentle but insistent resonance.

In *Thorn and Clegyr Boia*, the thorn tree at front right becomes an interplay of fragmented lines on the picture surface, pulsing with movement, a vivid formal pattern which also suggests a nearby tree moving in the wind seen out of the corner of the eye whilst looking into the distance at something else. So the focus of the painting is the far humped mass of Clegyr Boia, a steep-sided Pembrokeshire hill rising above the plain, and the site of Neolithic and Iron Age settlements. But the foreground activity (which here includes a blocky collaged band breaking the rectangle to the left and again along the lower edge) is what at first captures the viewer's attention. Ultimately, the painting is about

11 There Is Still Gorse (Winter, Garn Fawr), 2011 mixed media on paper 59 x 78 cms 23¼ x 30¾ ins Pembrokeshire

12 The Year Ending. Clegyr Boia I, 2014 mixed media on paper 47 x 70 cms 18½ x 27½ ins Pembrokeshire

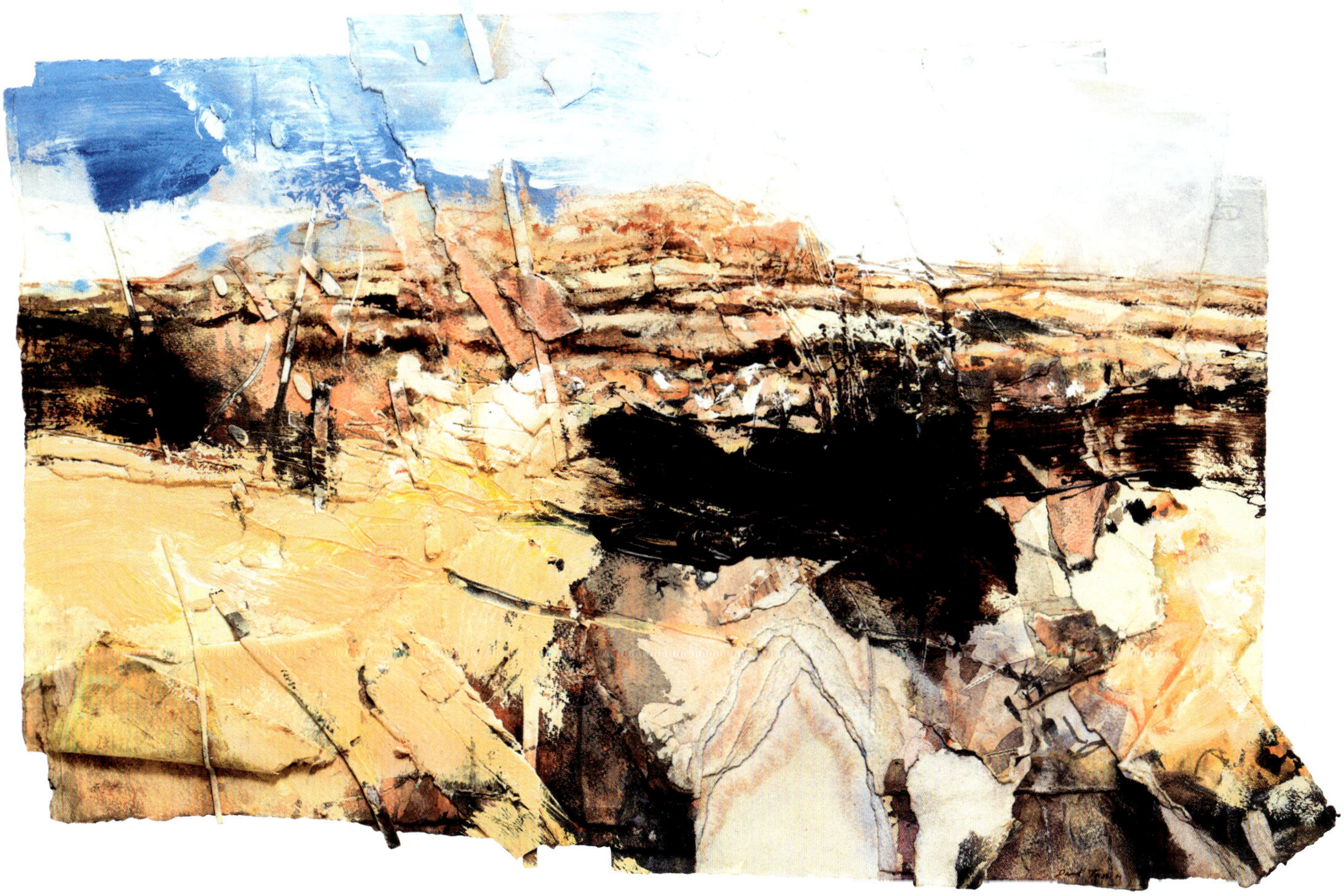

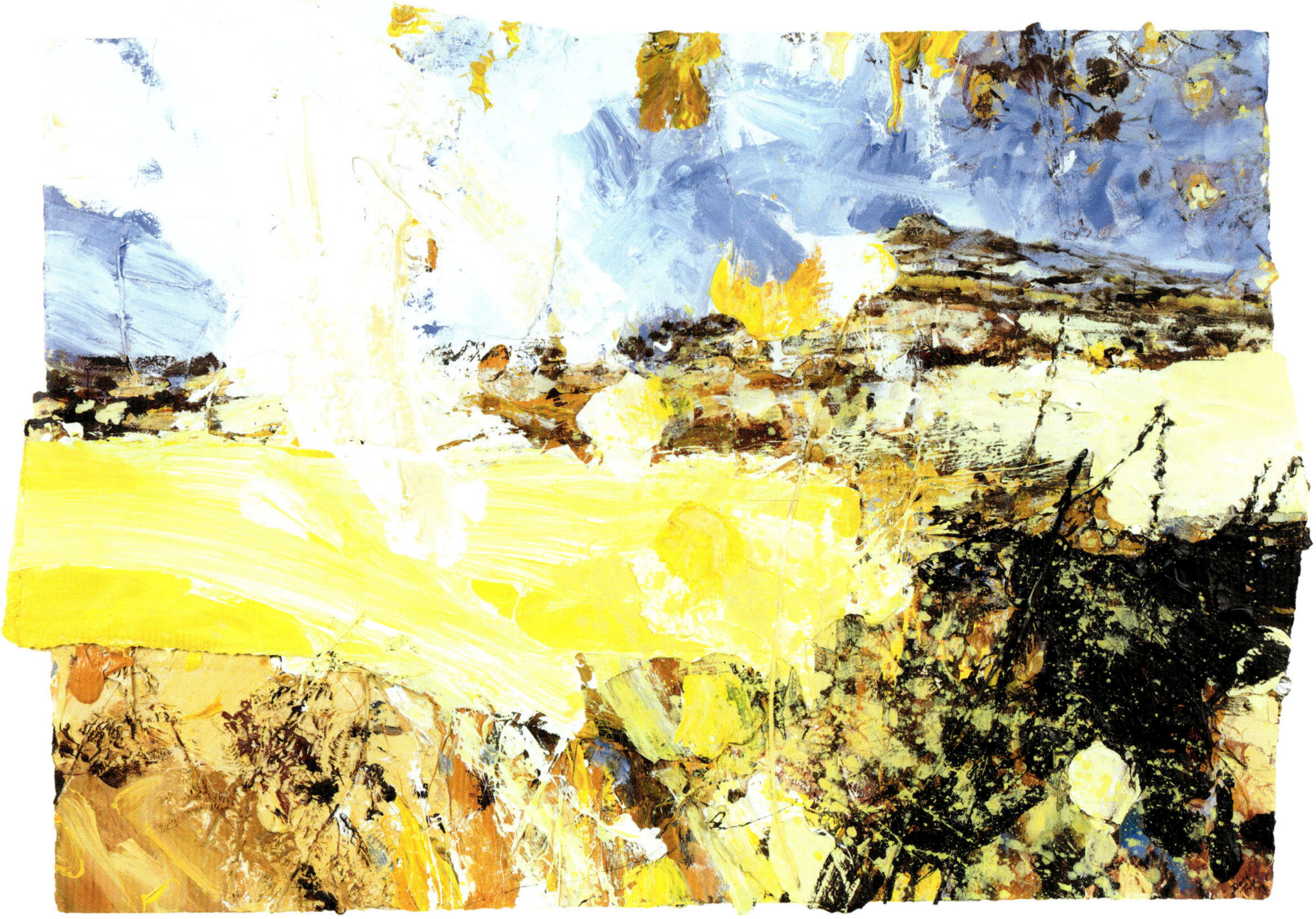

the dialogue between foreground and background, about how we see things (or don't notice them) close to us at the same time as far away. Also about how we often take things around us for granted (foreground blur and fragmented detail). The artist's skill lies in uniting these disparate visual and conceptual impulses.

It gives me great pleasure to congratulate David on his remarkable achievement to date, and to wish him not only A Very Happy Birthday but many more productive years ahead.

Andrew Lambirth
Author and Art Critic
March 2015

13 Sun I Saw on This Day (Carn Llidi), 2013 mixed media on paper 81 x 118 cms 31⅞ x 46½ ins Pembrokeshire

14 Green Hill (Wet Spring), 2014 mixed media on paper 66 x 82 cms 26 x 32¼ ins Pembrokeshire

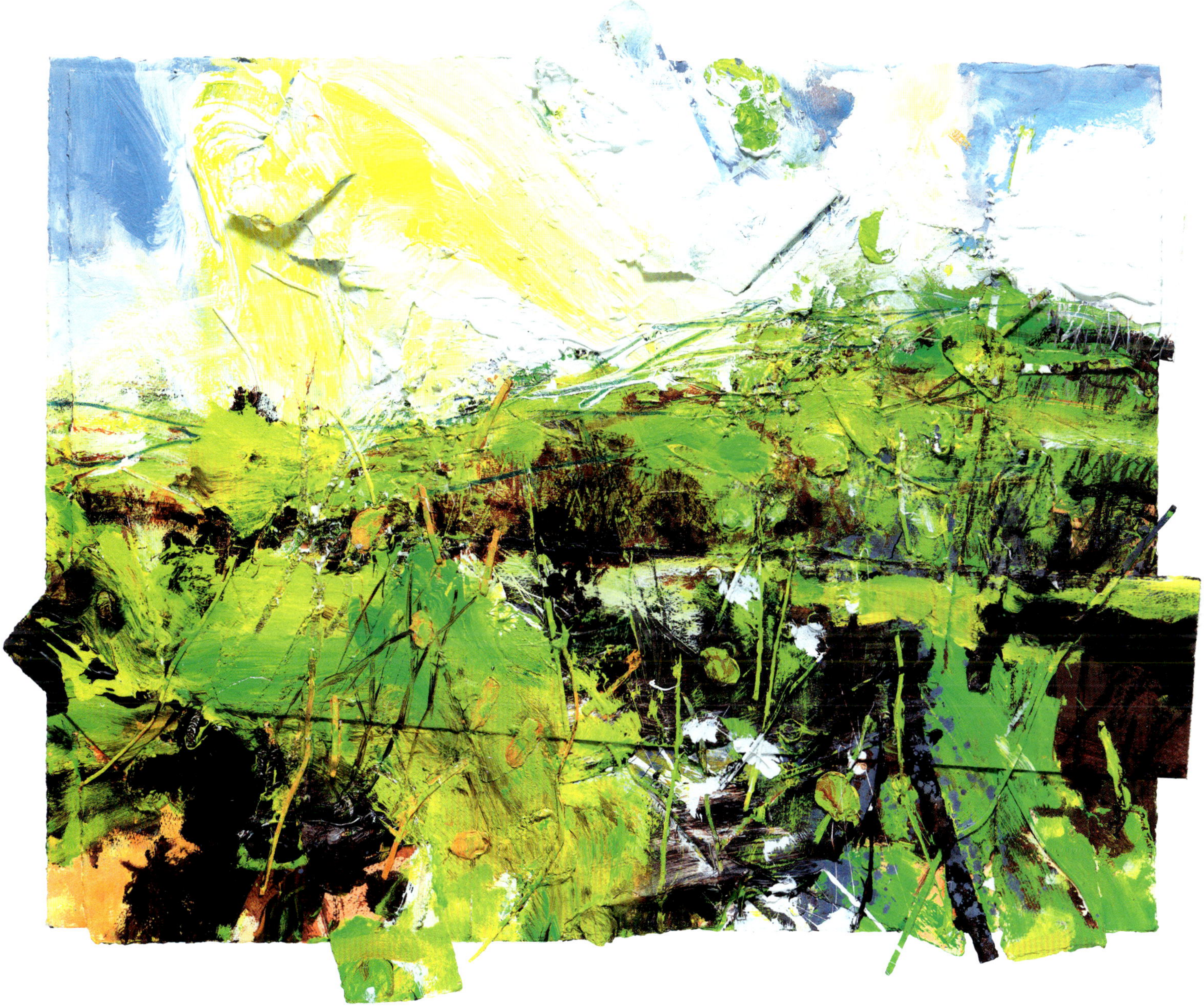

15 Red Hill, Early Light (Llanthony), 2011 mixed media on paper 40 x 57 cms 15¾ x 22½ ins Monmouthshire

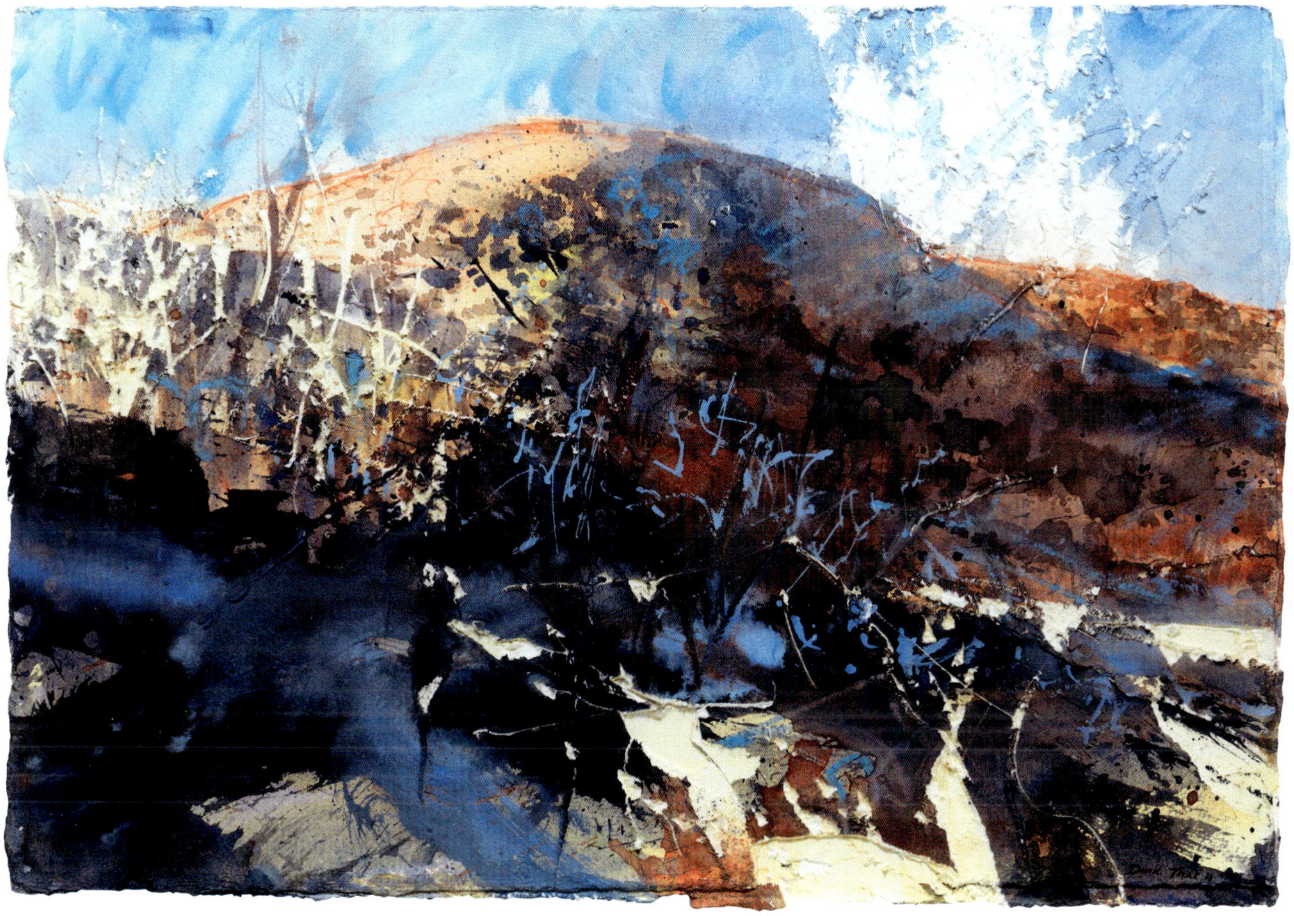

16 Llanthony Valley, Winter Sun, 2014 mixed media on paper 46 x 64 cms 18⅛ x 25¼ ins Monmouthshire

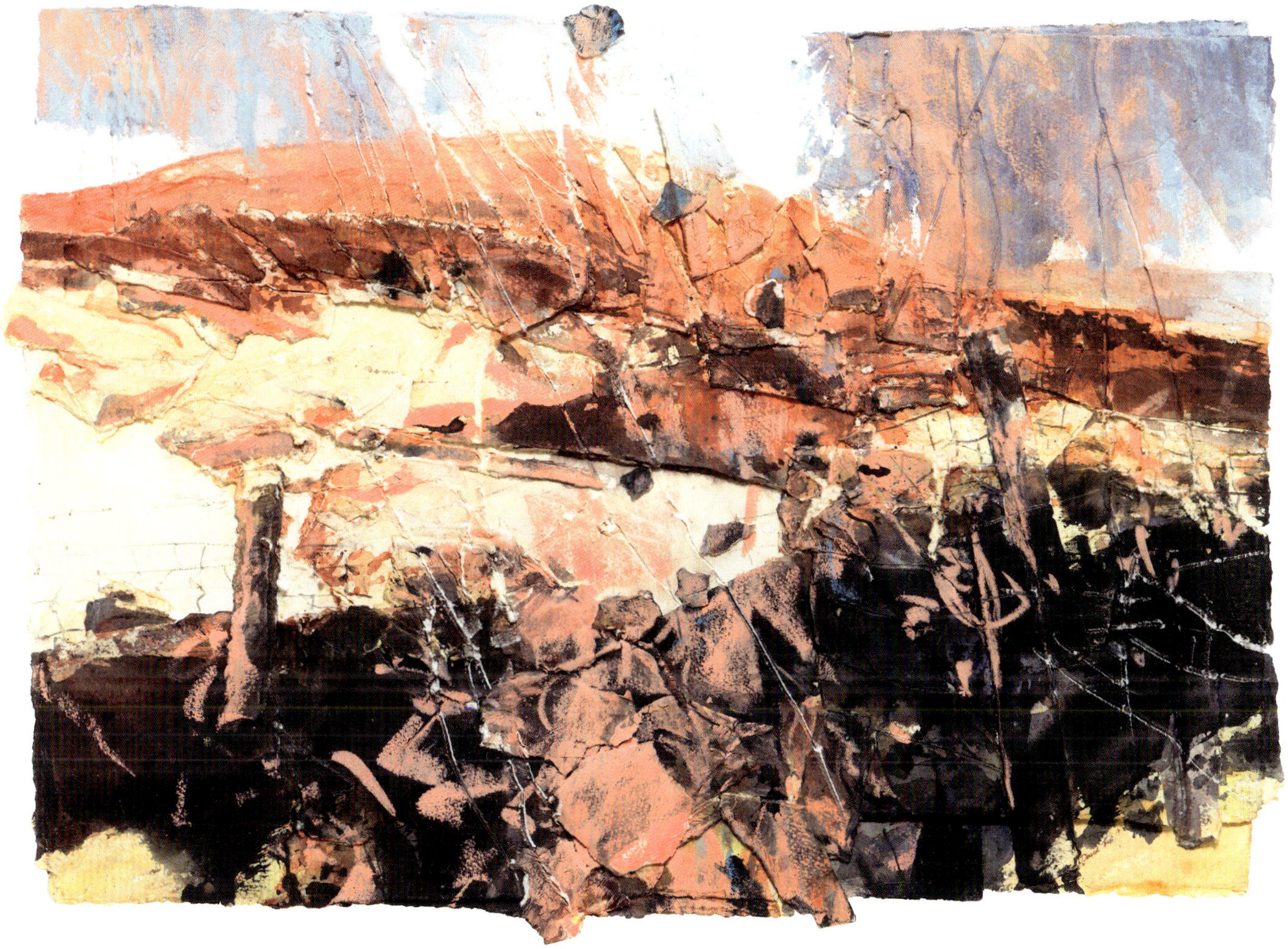

17 Brief Sun (November), 2010 mixed media on paper 40 x 58 cms 15¾ x 22⅞ ins Pembrokeshire

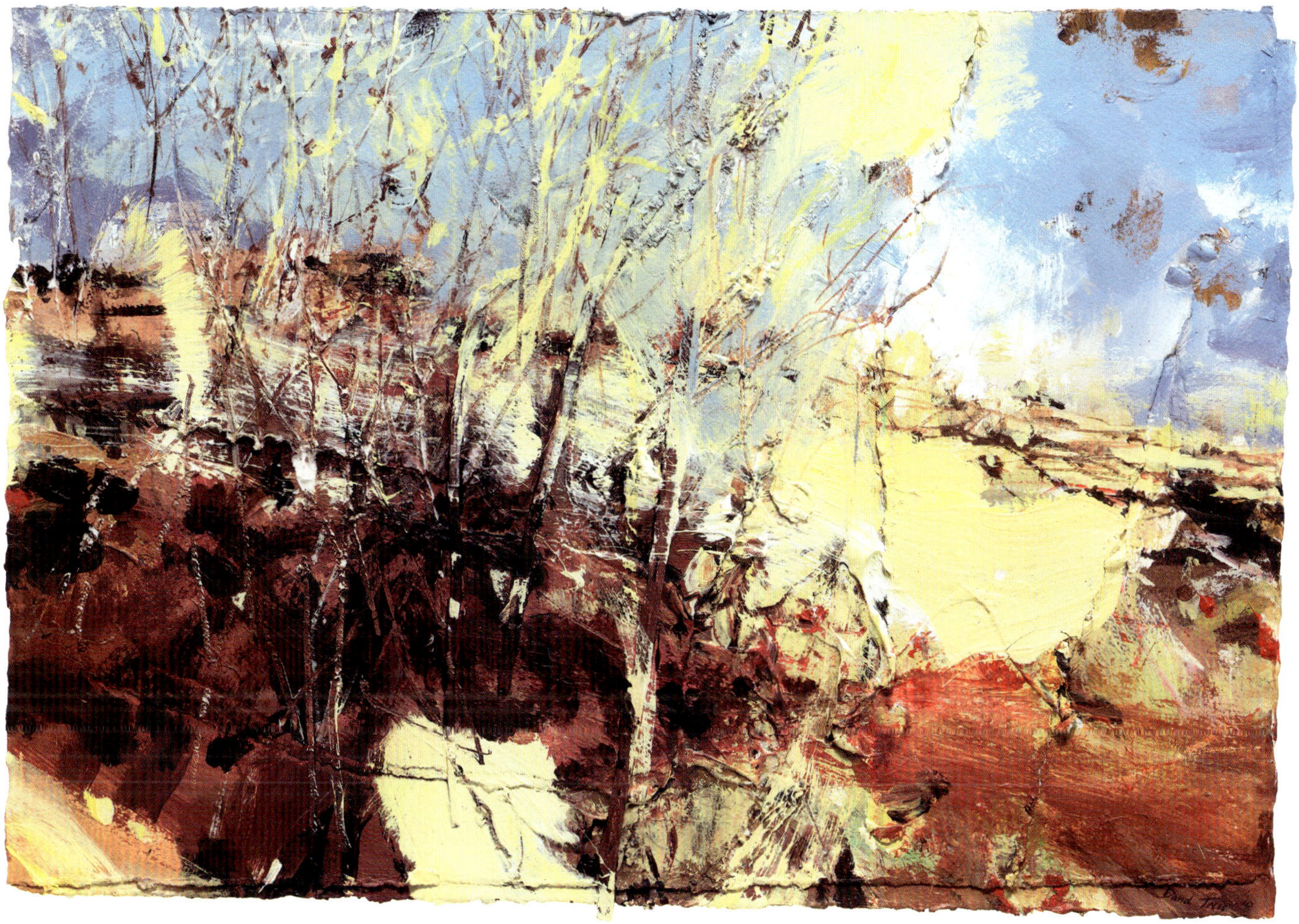

18 Thorn and Clegyr Boia, 2014 mixed media on paper 64 x 86 cms 25¼ x 33⅞ ins Pembrokeshire

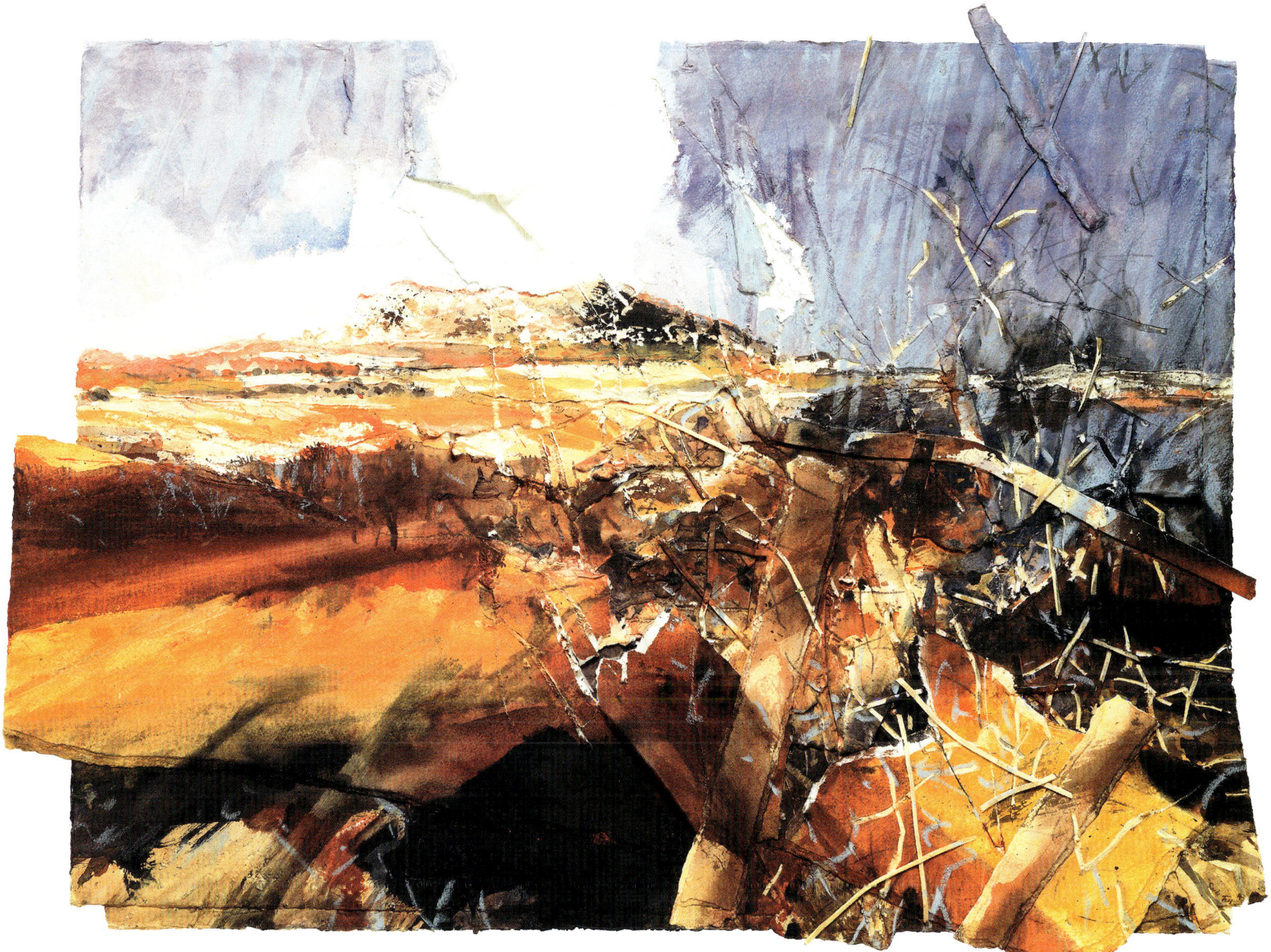

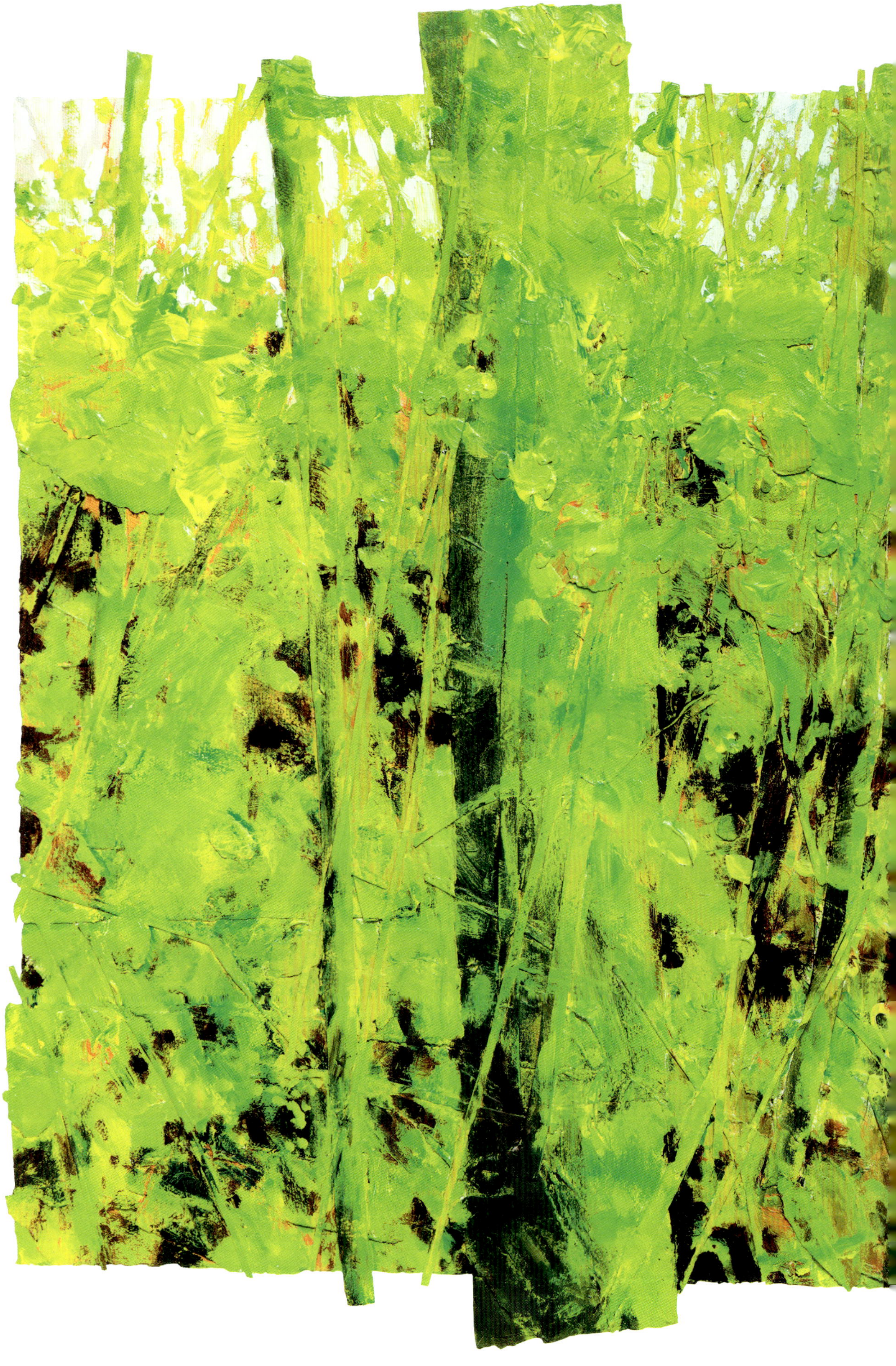

19 Green Spring Valley Bud Burst, 2014 mixed media on paper 94 x 134 cms 37 x 52¾ ins Pembrokeshire

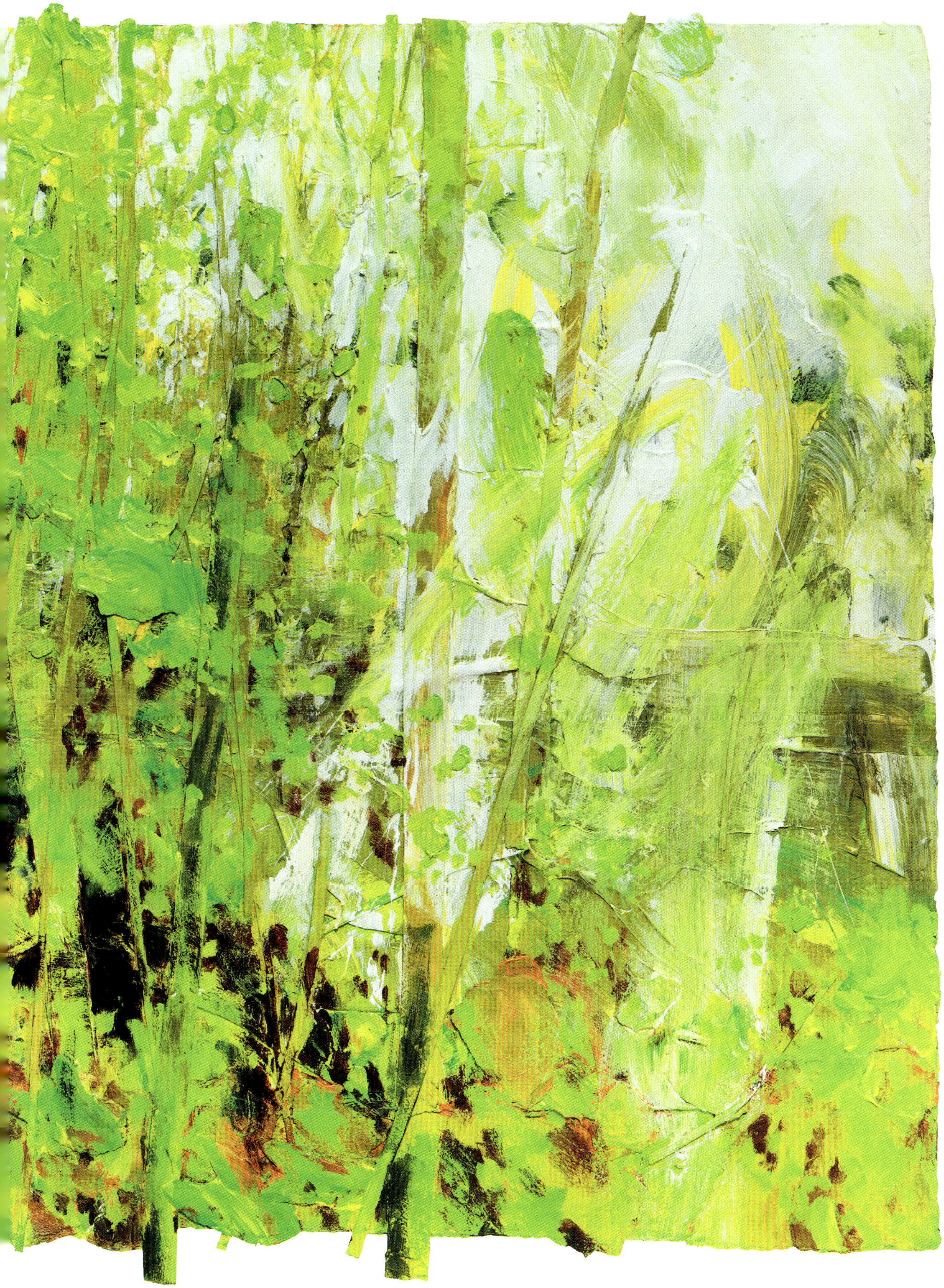

20 Now in November (Hazel) I, 2010 mixed media on paper 42 x 58 cms 16½ x 22⅞ ins Pembrokeshire

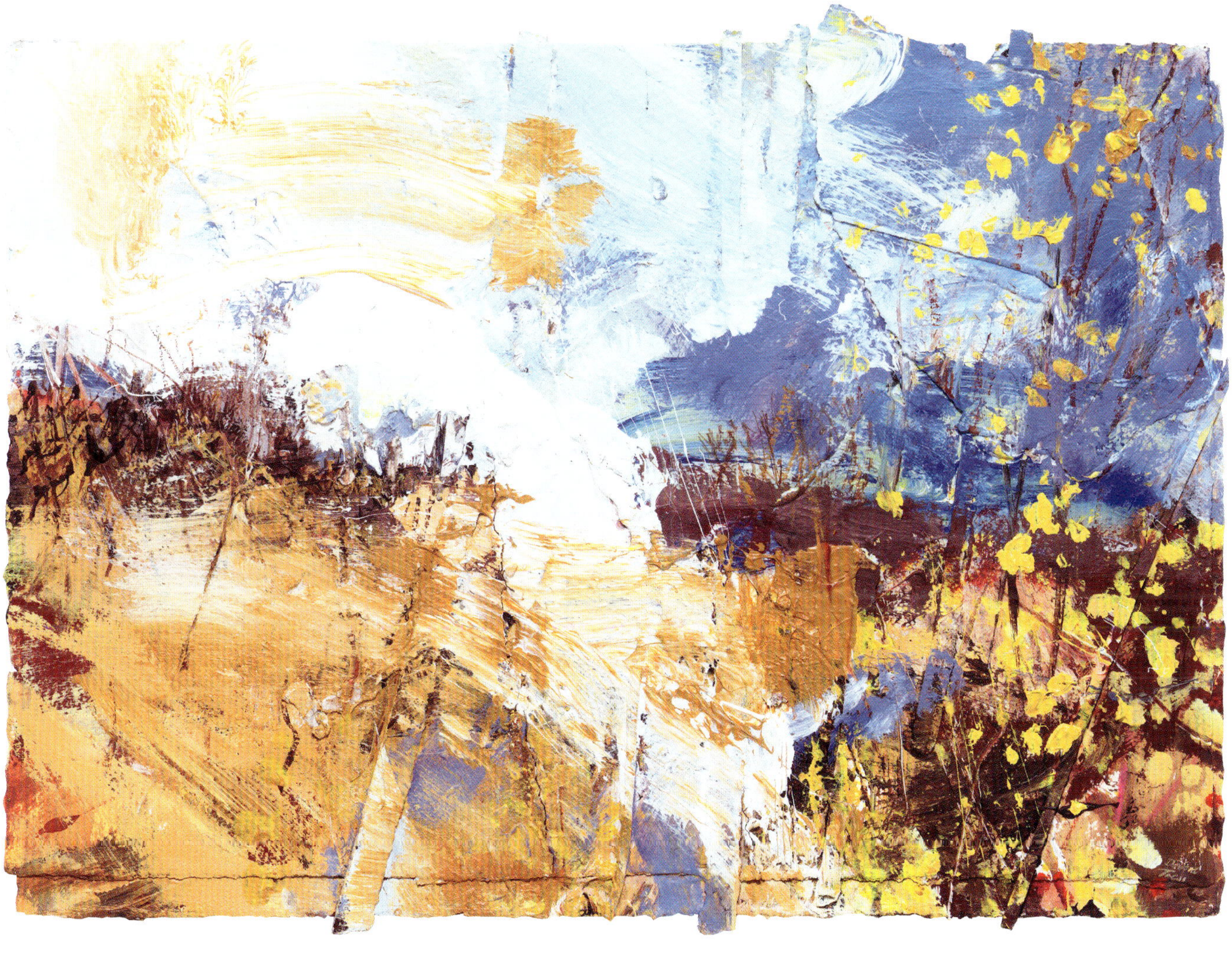

21 Is This Spring? (Trefeiddan Moor), 2013 mixed media on paper 61 x 84 cms 24 x 33⅛ ins Pembrokeshire

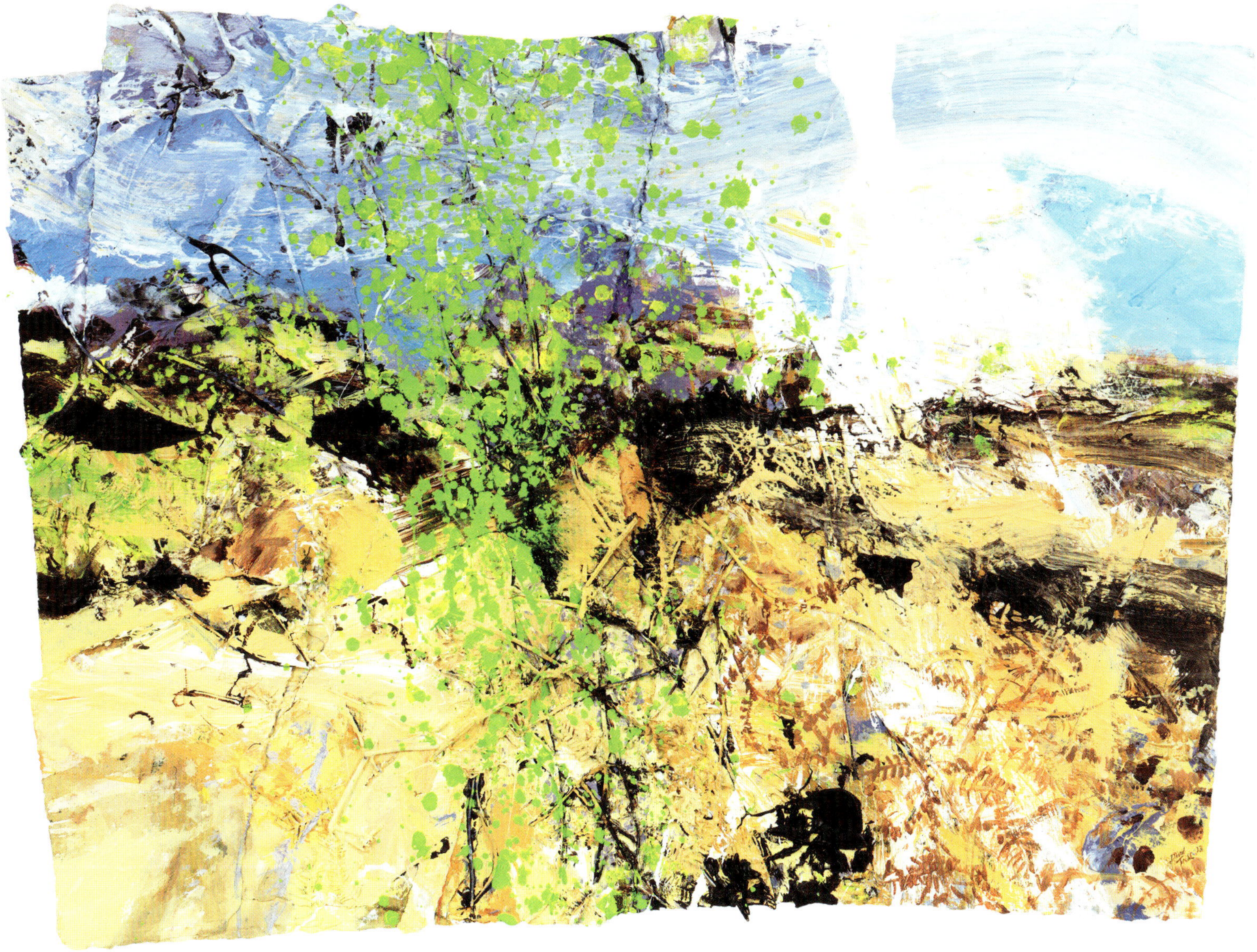

22 The Year Ending. Clegyr Boia II, 2014 mixed media on paper 60 x 70 cms 23⅝ x 27½ ins Pembrokeshire

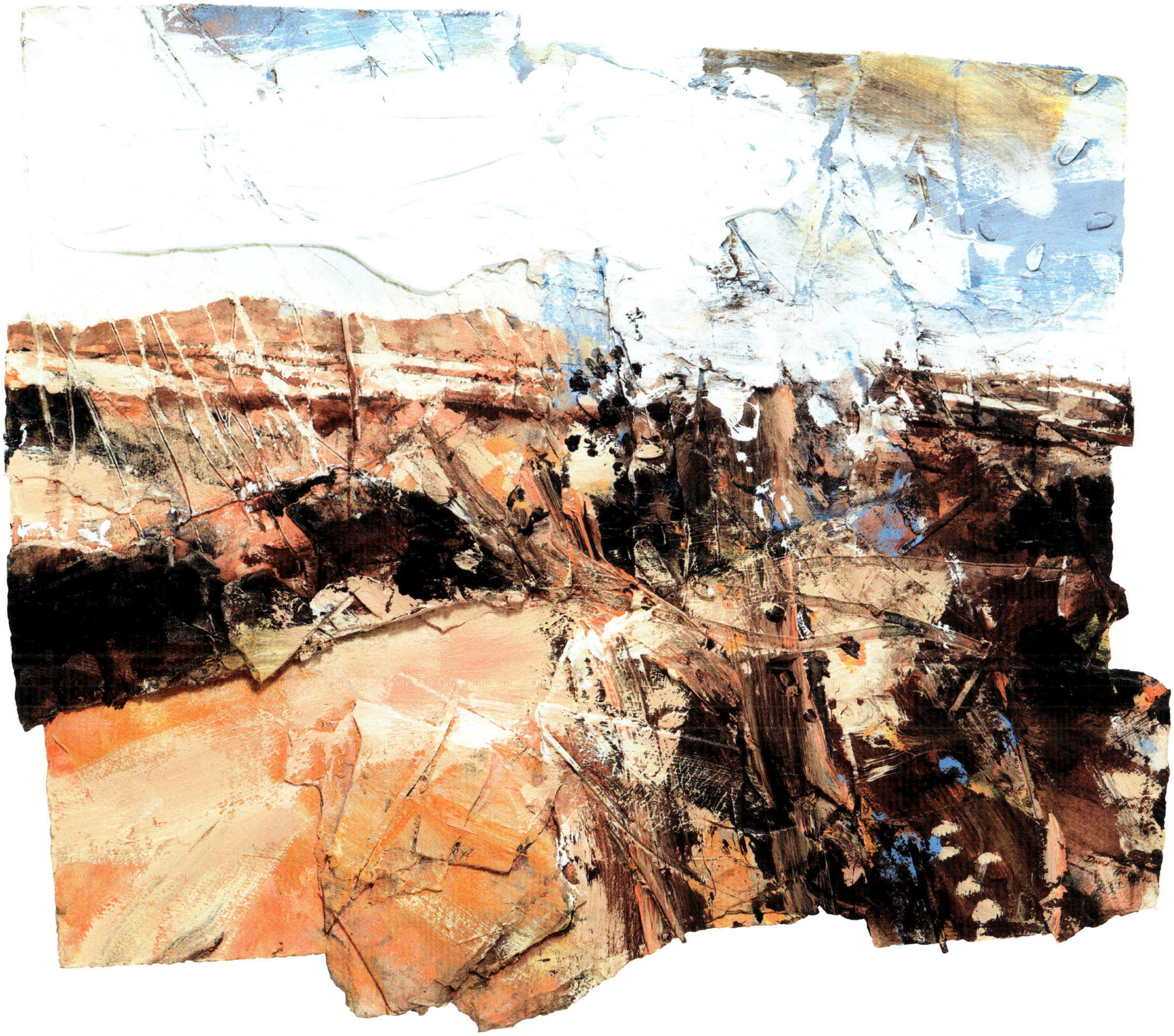

23 Ah Yes, Already Winter (Carn Llidi), 2014 mixed media on paper 55 x 73 cms 21⅝ x 28¾ ins Pembrokeshire

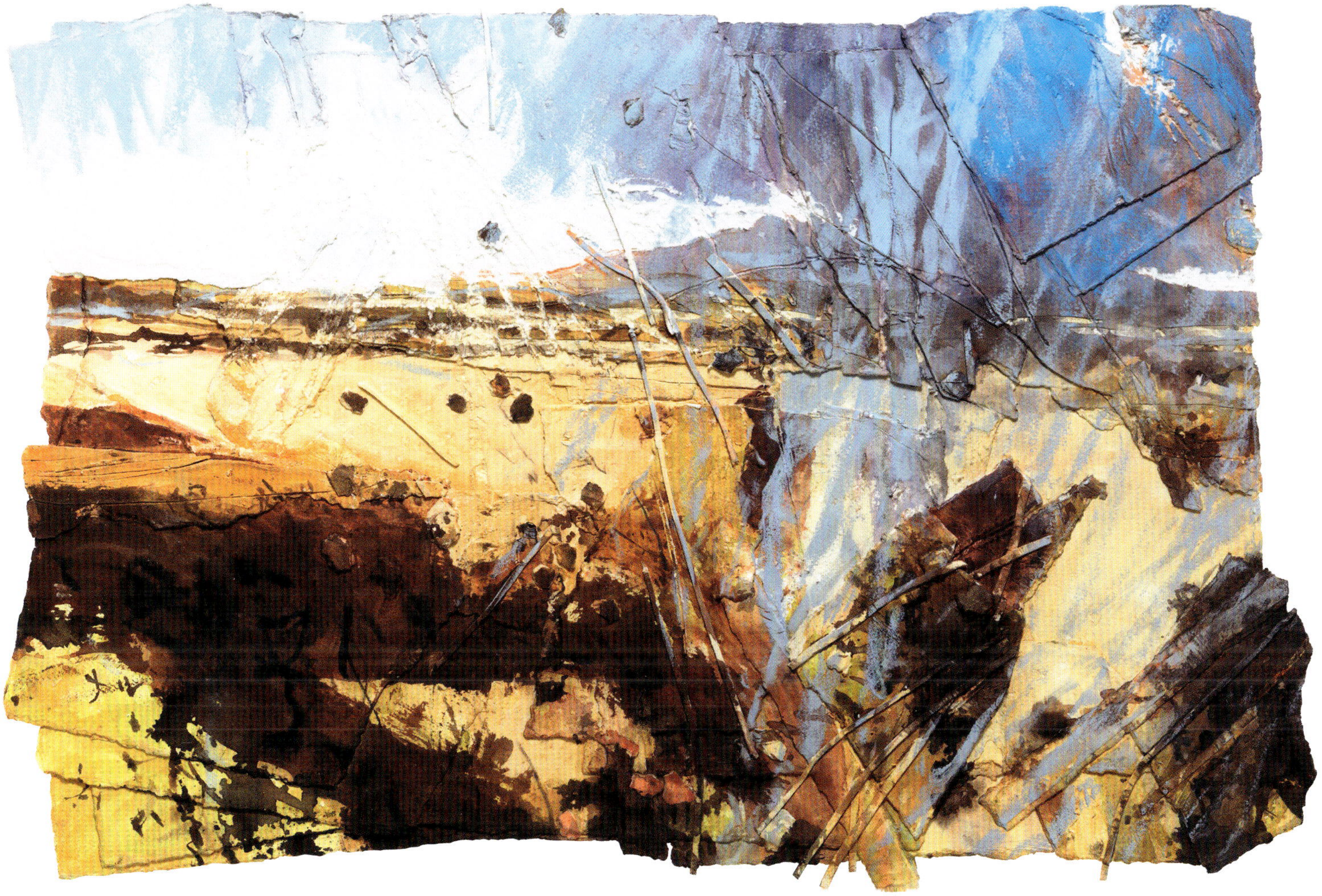

24 Two Hills, Winter (Carn Rhosson), 2014 mixed media on paper 62 x 69 cms 24⅜ x 27⅛ ins Pembrokeshire

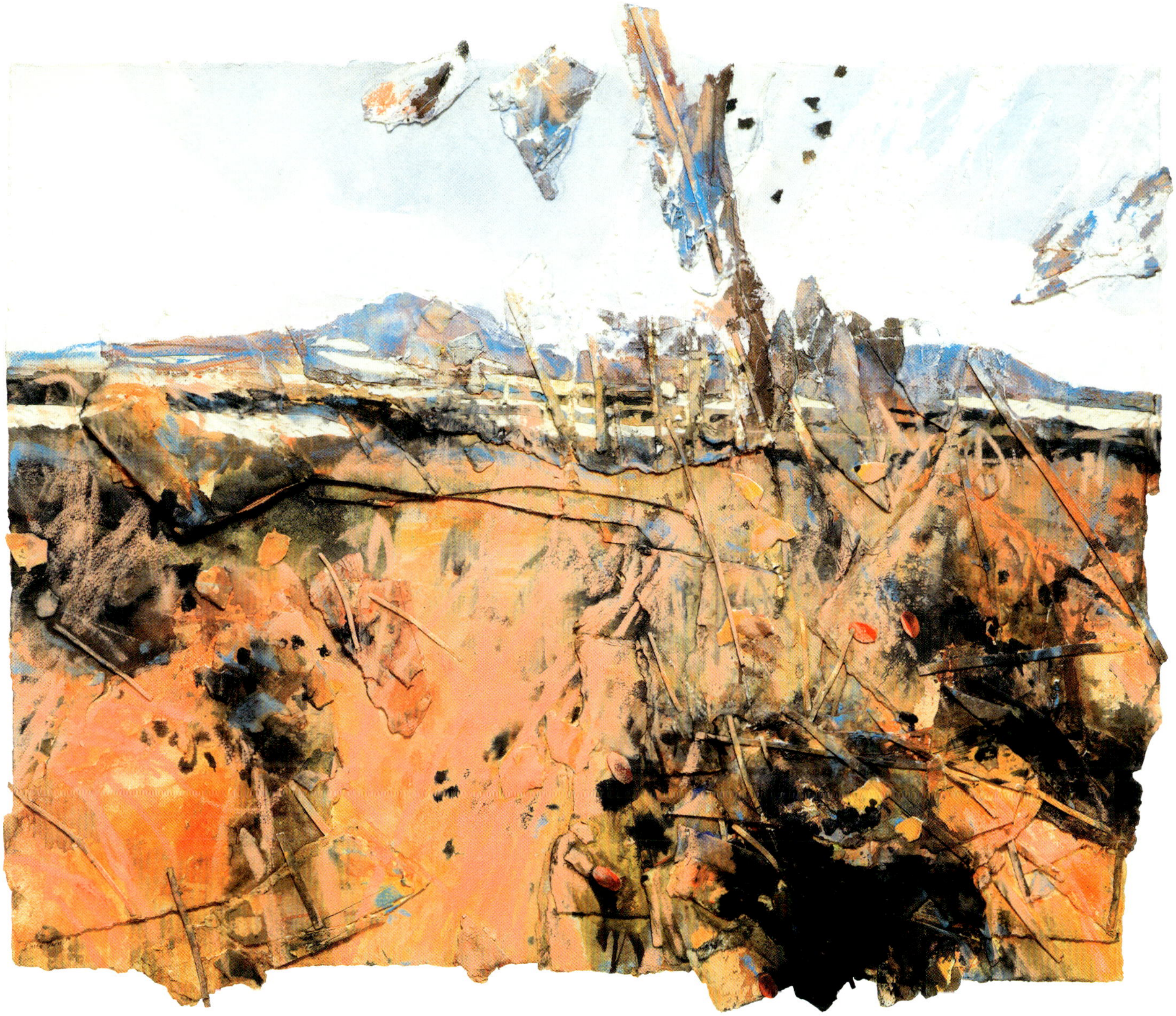

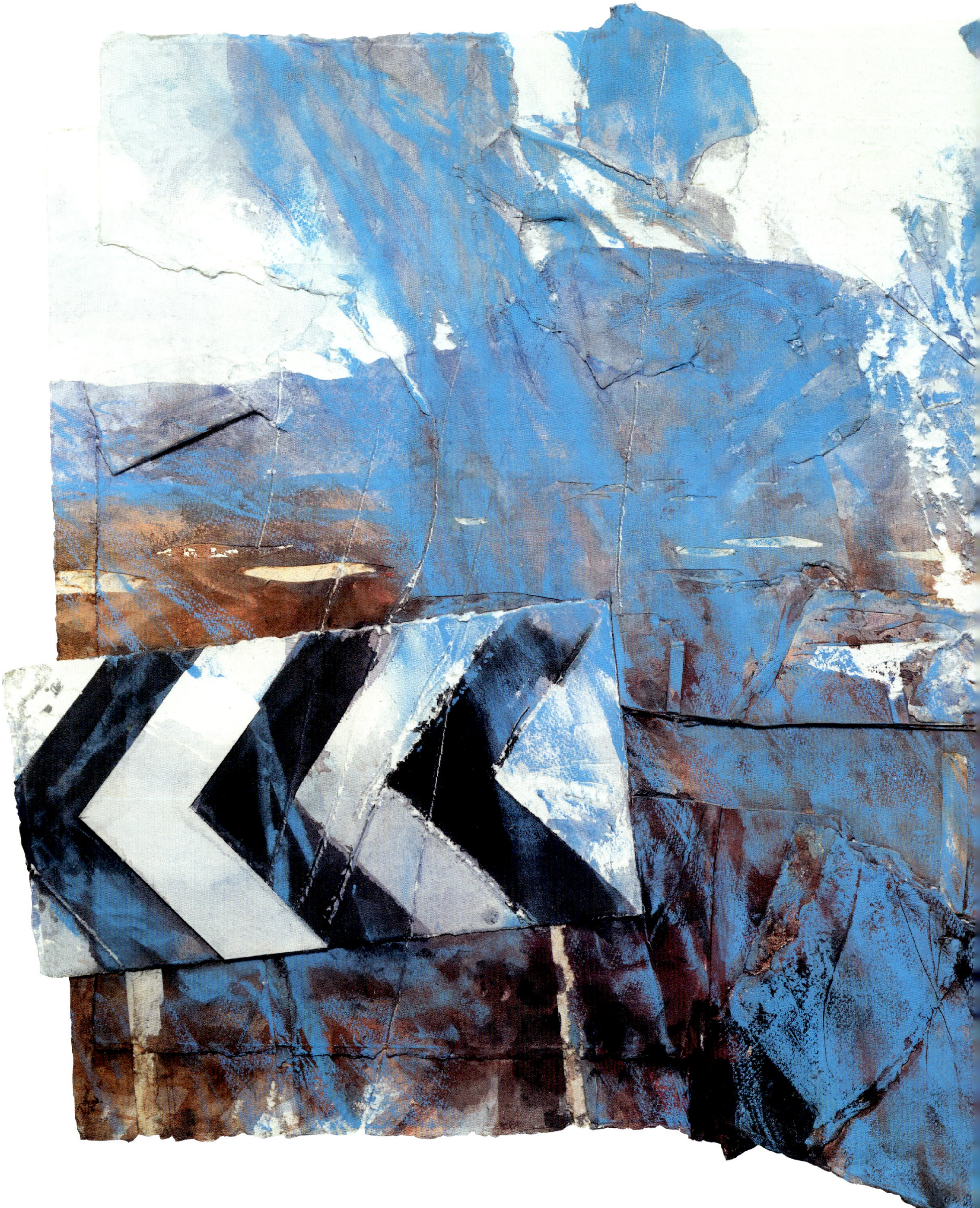

25 Turn Left For Muckish (Donegal), 2014 mixed media on paper 71 x 118 cms 28 x 46½ ins Ireland

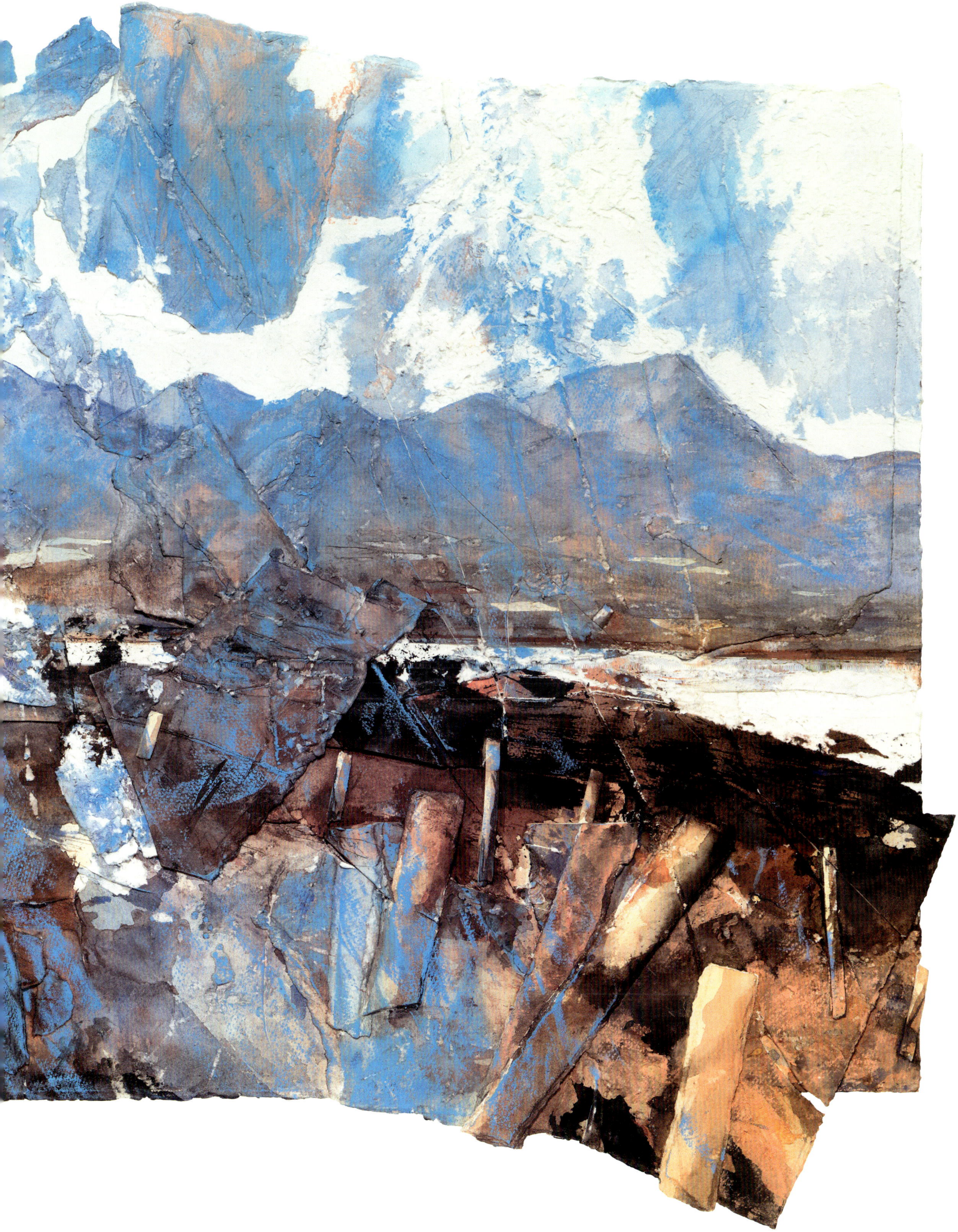

 Ah Yes, Ah Yes, Far Bodmin, 2013 mixed media on paper 60 x 83 cms 23⅝ x 32⅝ ins Cornwall

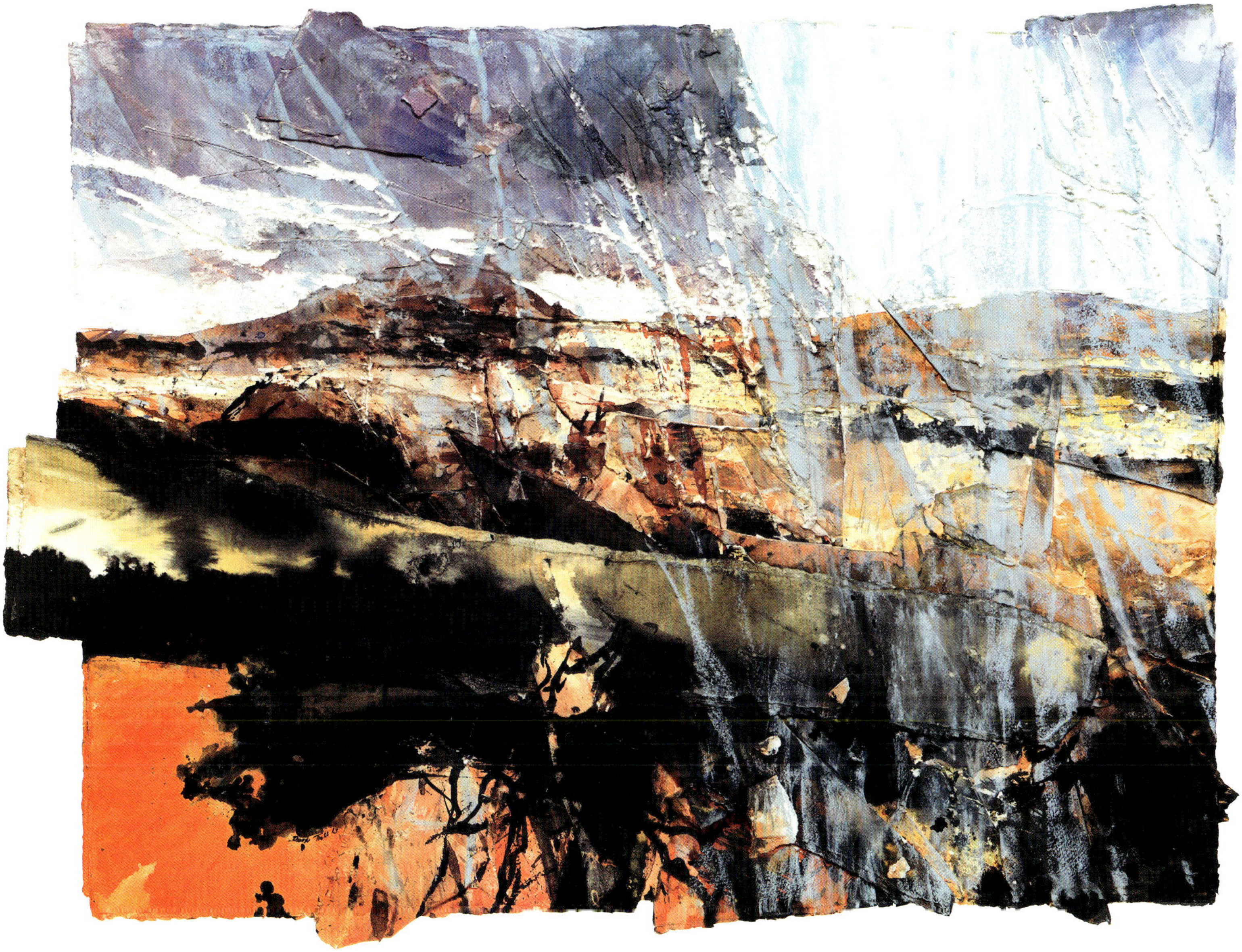

27 Ah Yes, Ah Yes, Bodmin (Garrow Tor), 2013 mixed media on paper 42 x 64 cms 16½ x 25¼ ins Cornwall

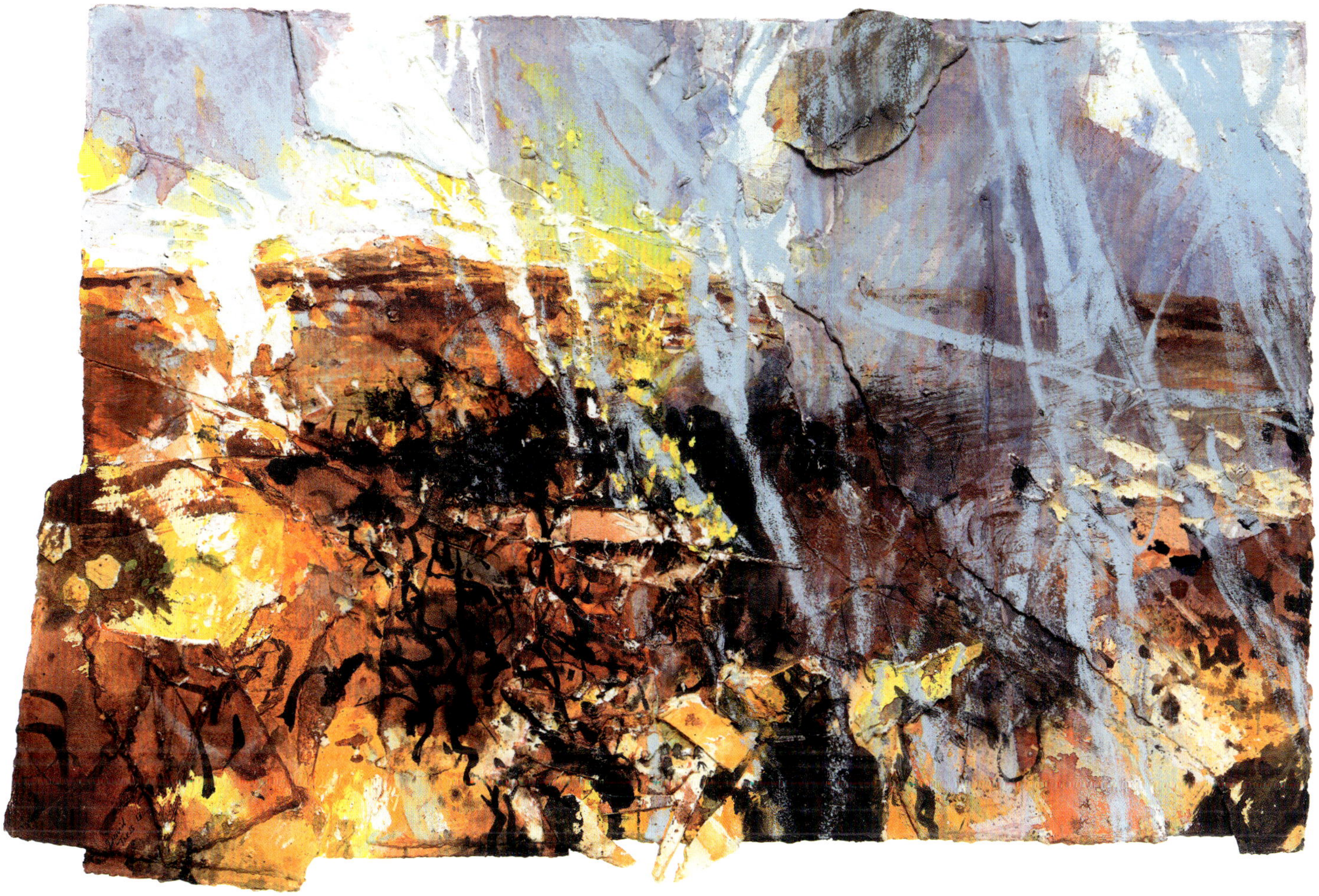

28 Fields Under Chun Down, 2014 mixed media on paper 46 x 60 cms 18⅛ x 23⅝ ins Cornwall

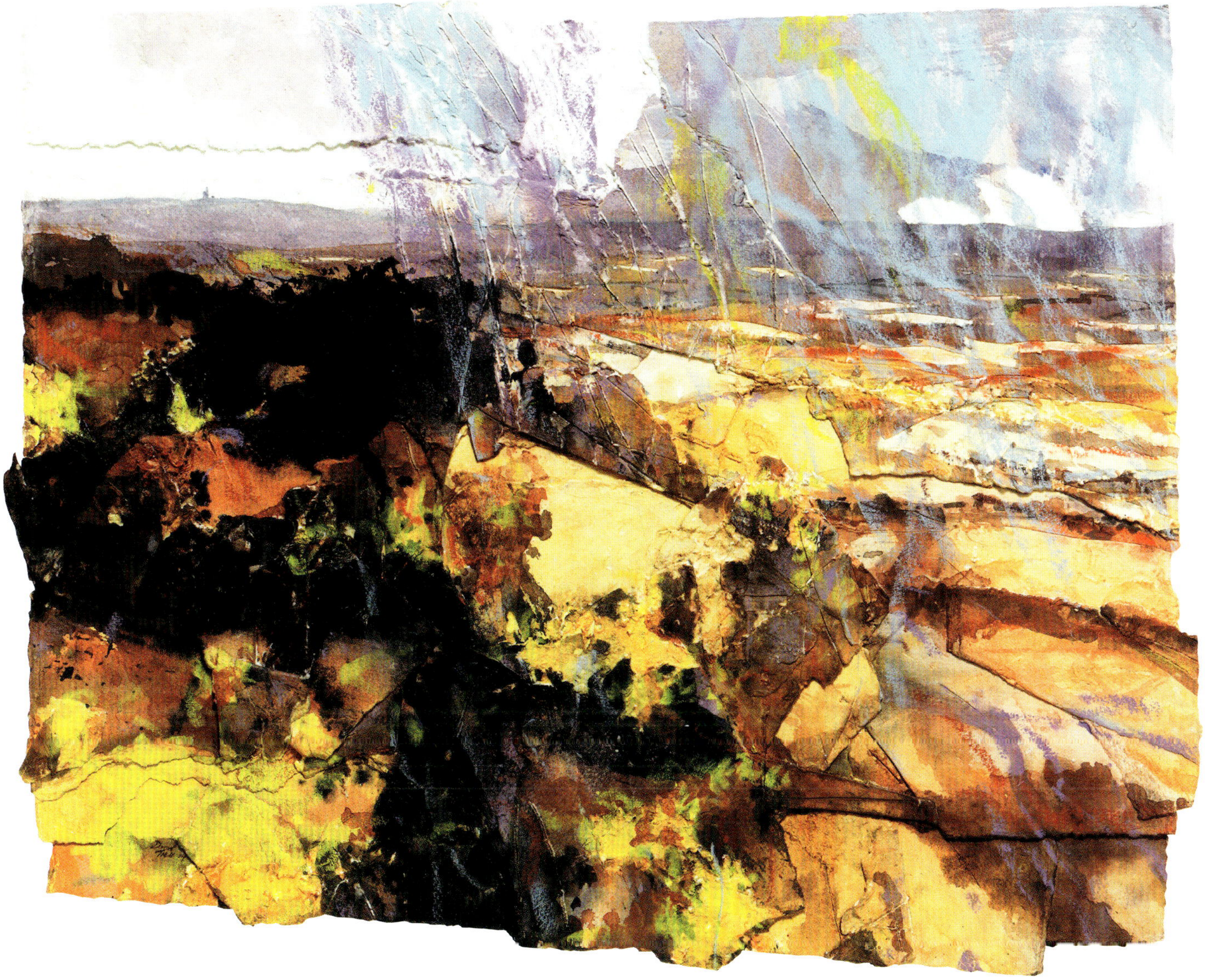

29 Fields and Sea (Near Gurnard's Head), 2014 mixed media on paper 50 x 63 cms 19⅝ x 24¾ ins Cornwall

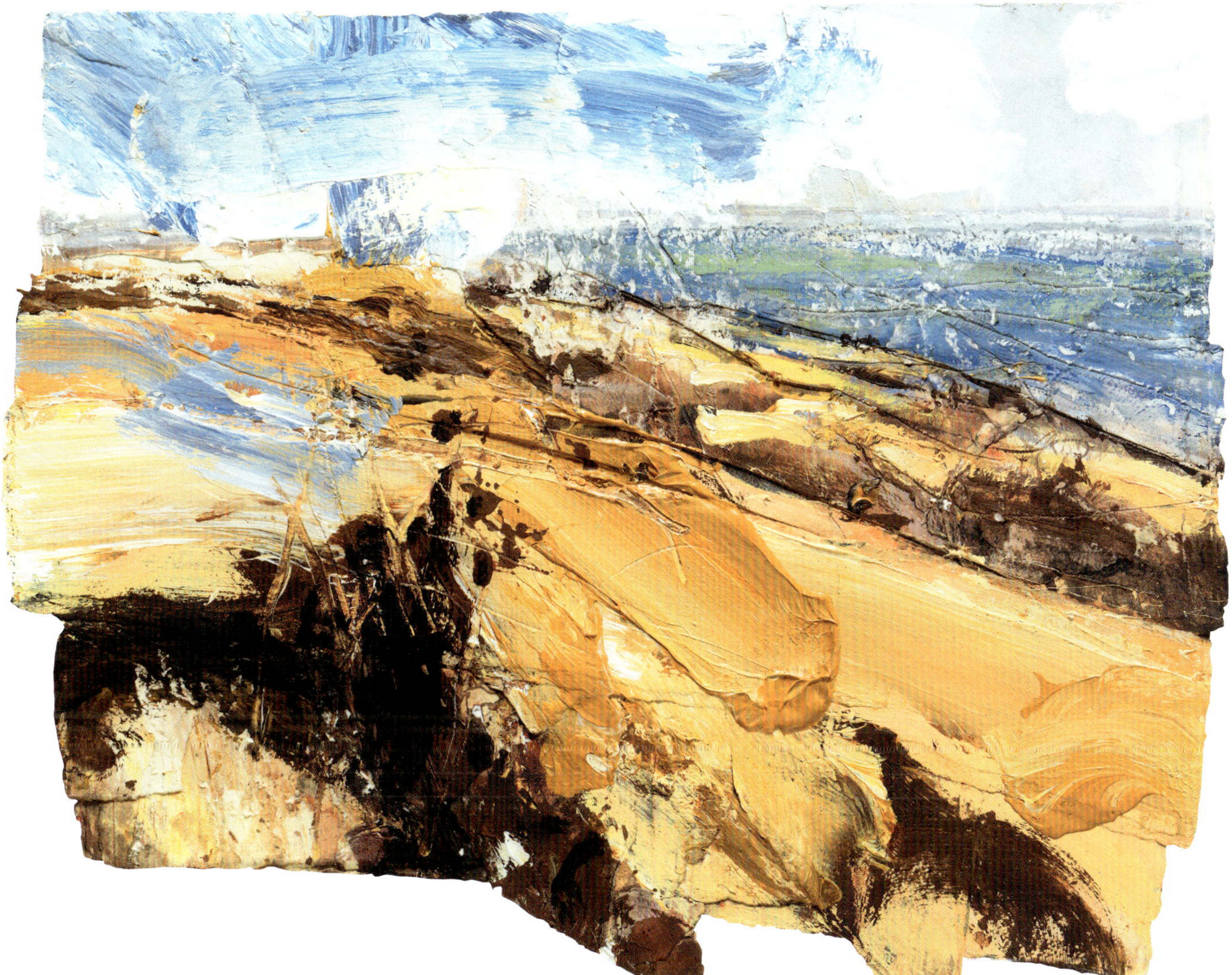

30 Zennor Hill, Red, 2014 mixed media on paper 52 x 64 cms 20½ x 25¼ ins Cornwall

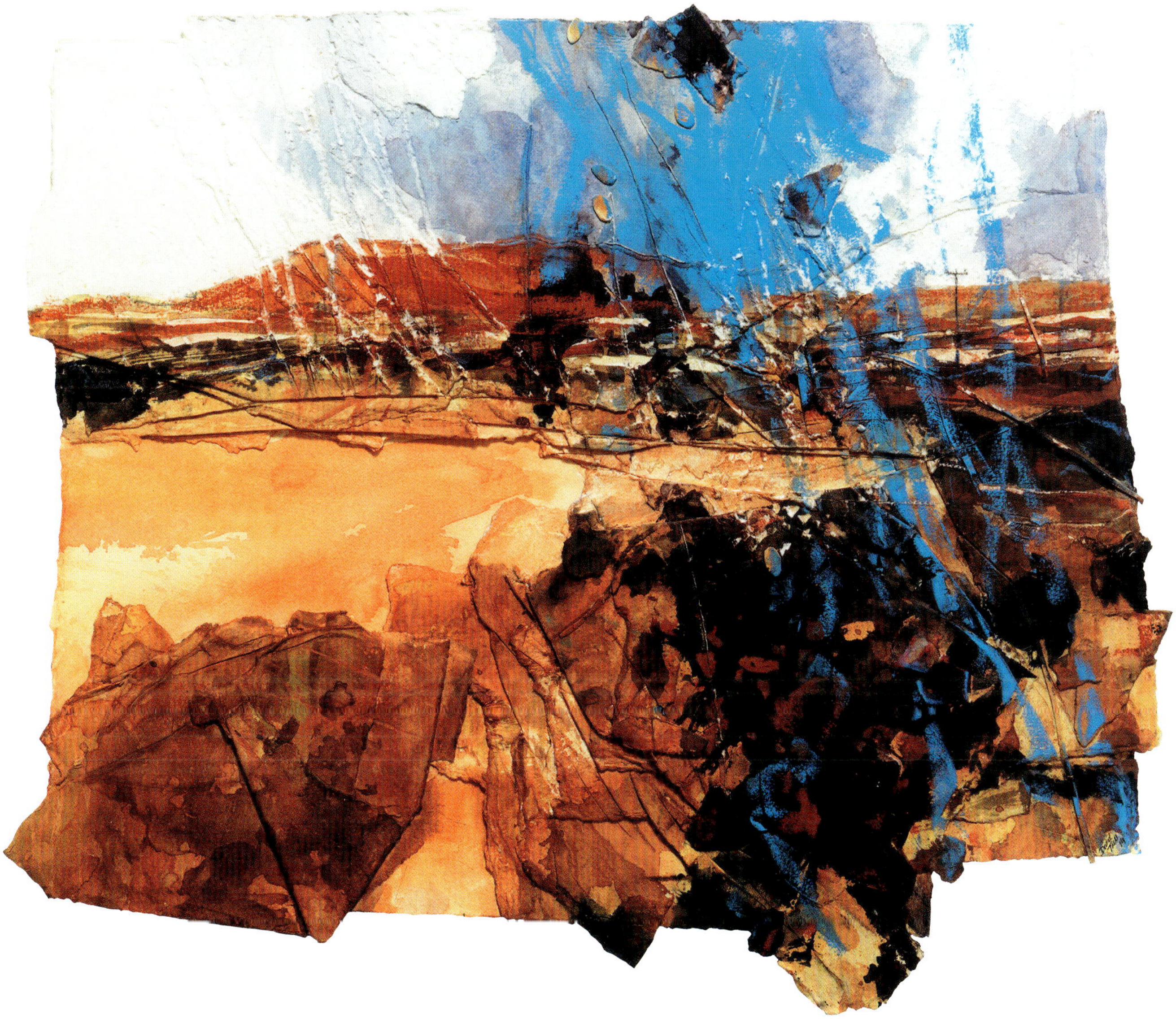

31 Trendrine, Autumn, 2014 mixed media on paper 54 x 58 cms 21¼ x 22⅞ ins Cornwall

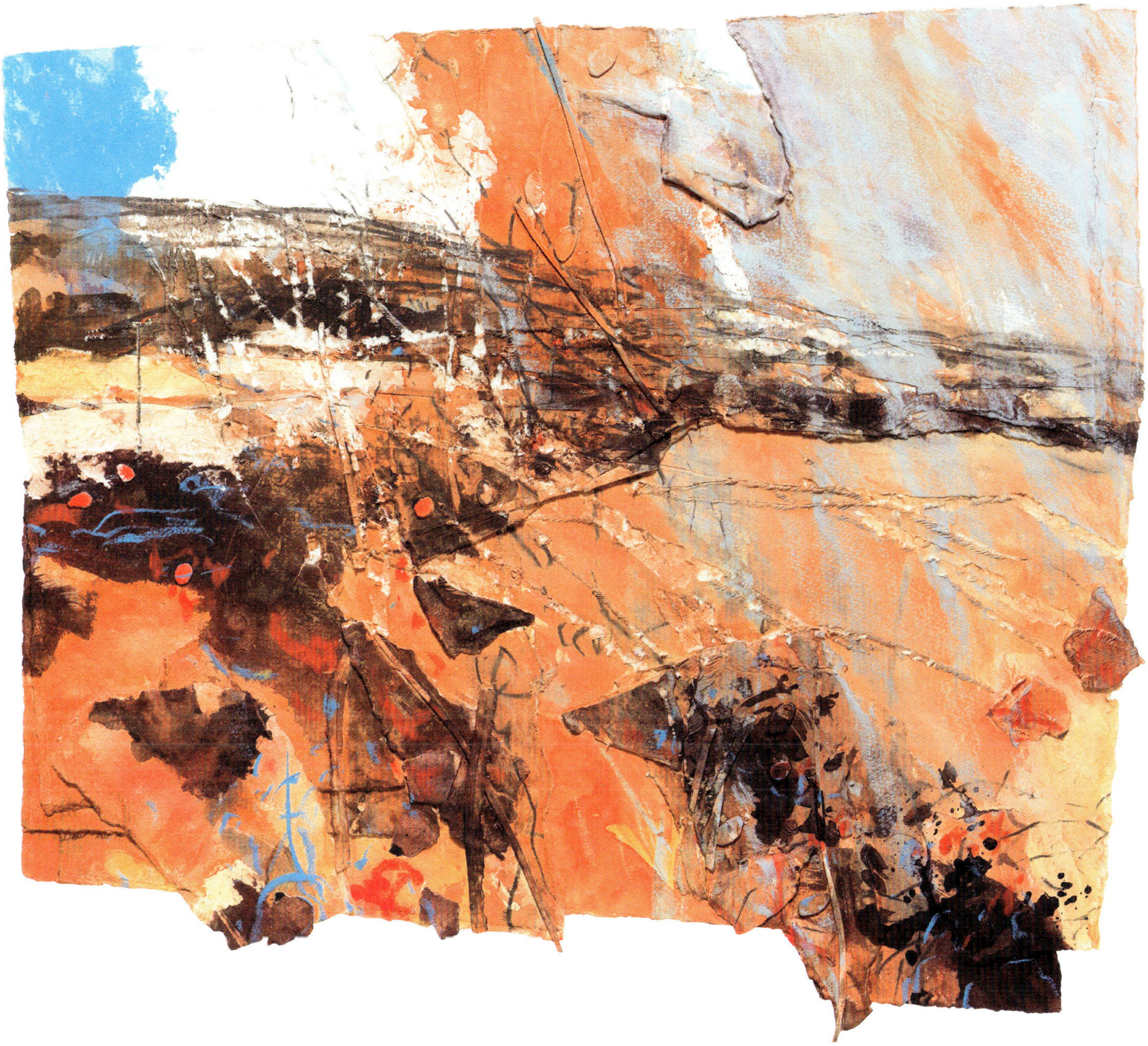

32 Little Trevalgan, 2014 mixed media on paper 50 x 61 cms 19⅝ x 24 ins Cornwall

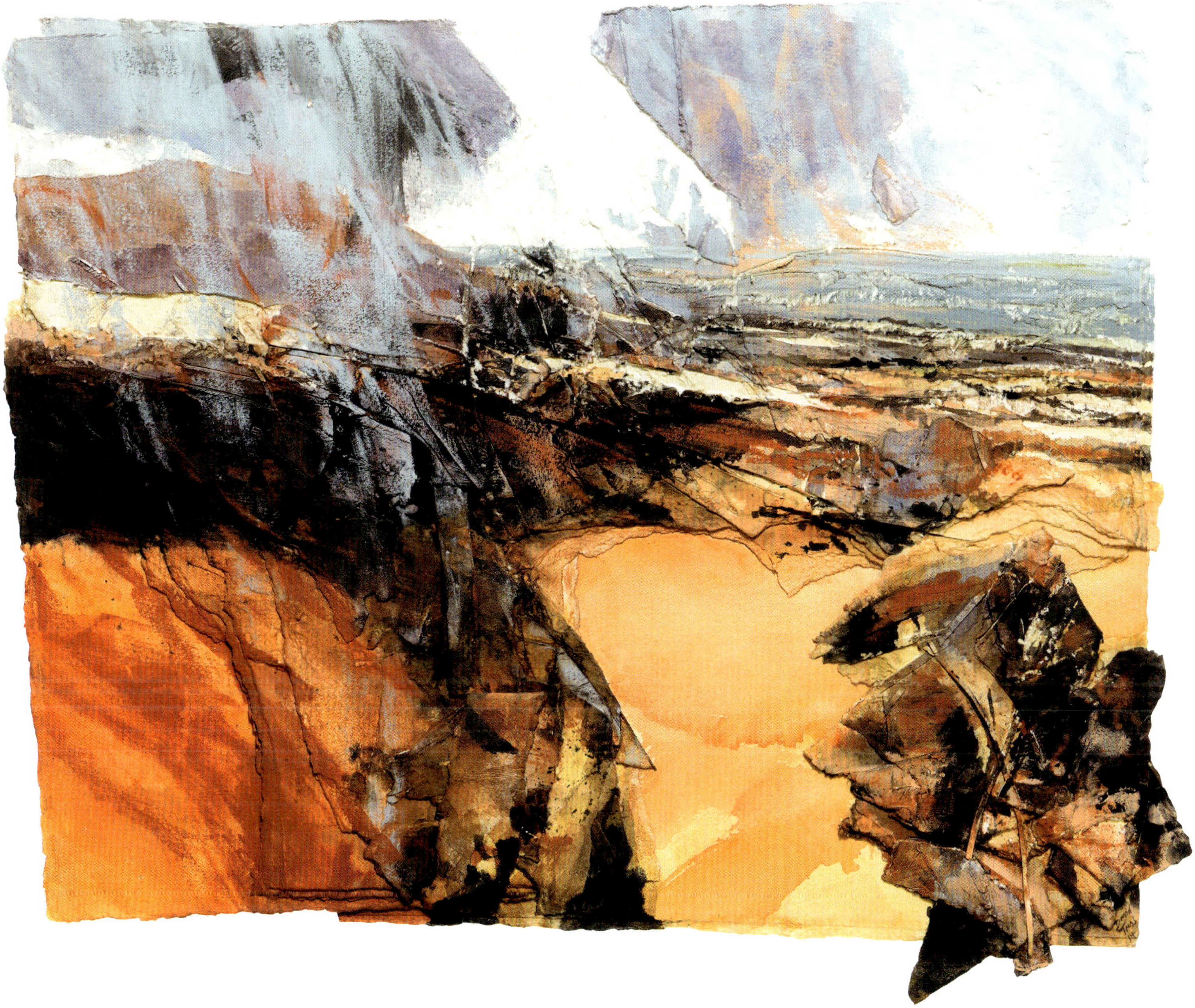

33 A Cool Day (Trevalga, Autumn), 2014 mixed media on paper 45 x 68 cms 17¾ x 26¾ ins Cornwall

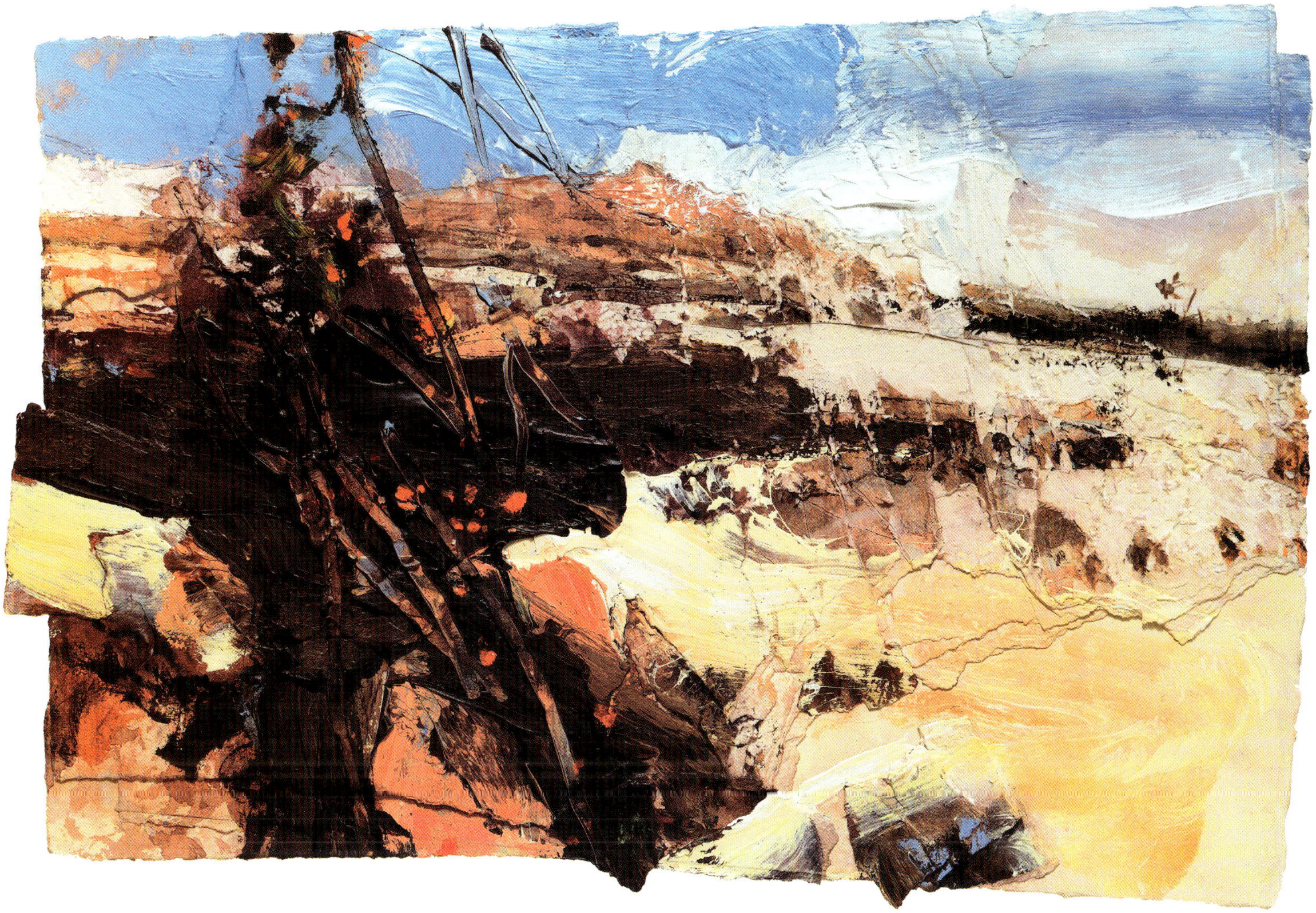

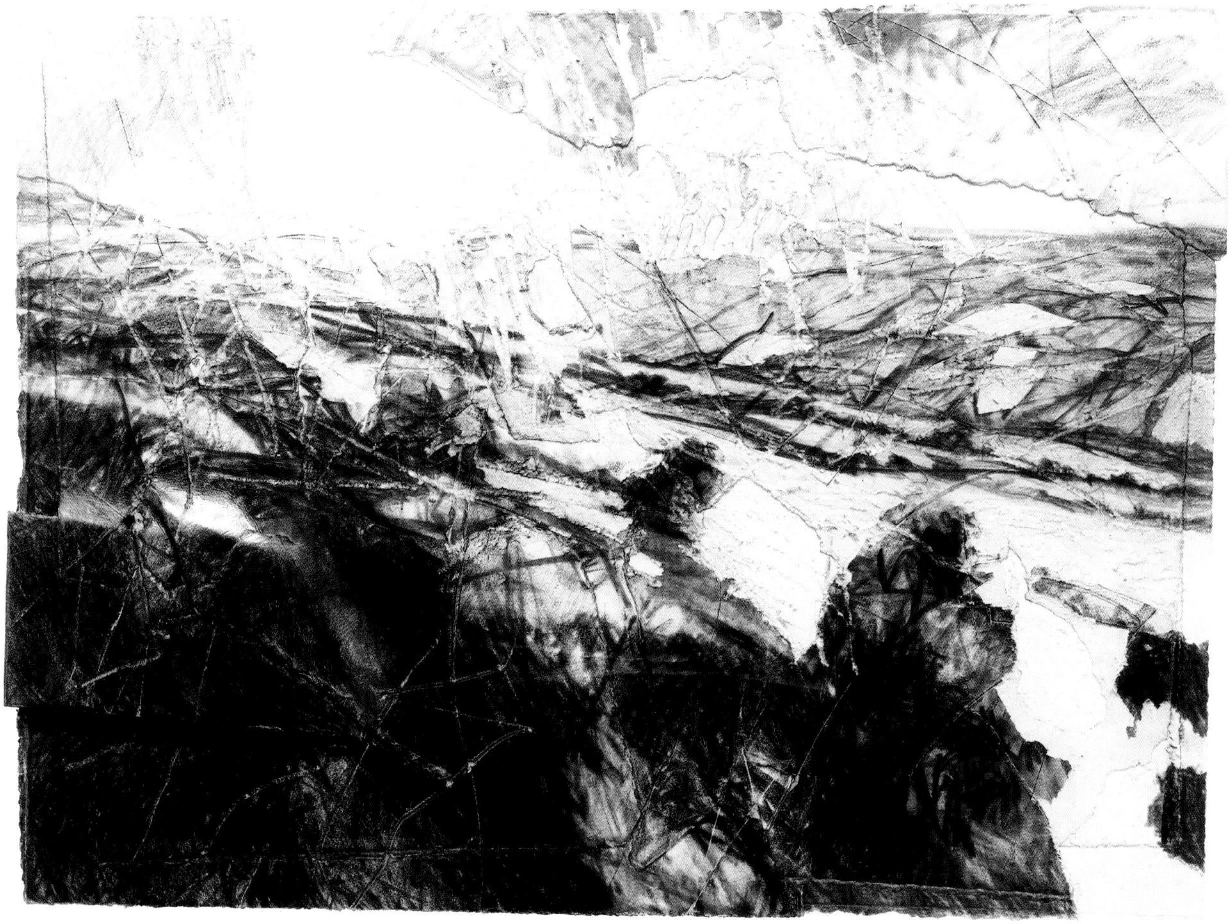

34 Hayfields, Eskdale, 2014 graphite on paper 65 x 87 cms 25⅝ x 34¼ ins Yorkshire

35 Green Eskdale Green, 2014 mixed media on paper 79 x 117 cms 31⅛ x 46⅛ ins Yorkshire

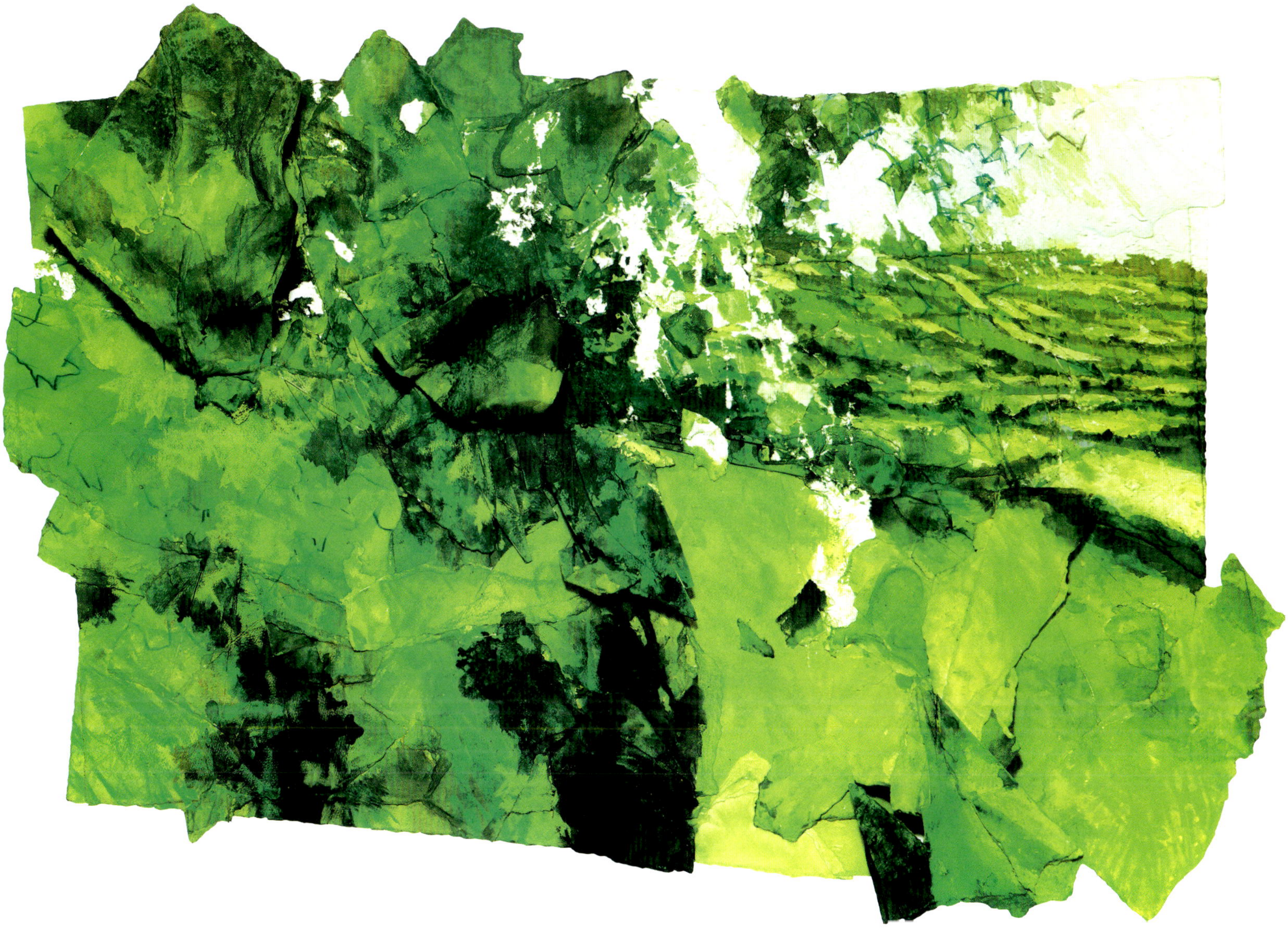

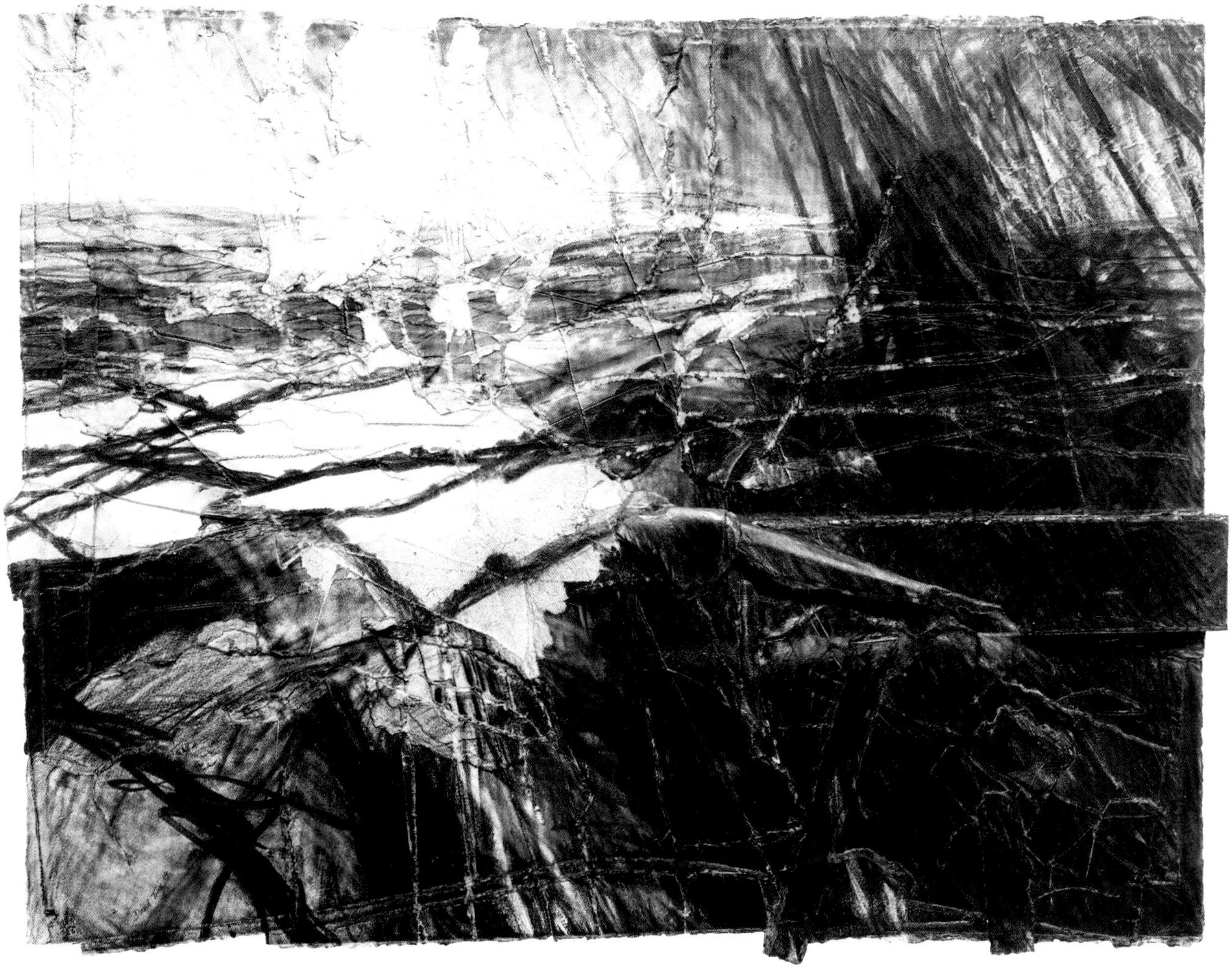

36 Rain in the Wind (Hayfields, Eskdale), 2014 graphite on paper 64 x 85 cms 25¼ x 33½ ins Yorkshire

37 Early Summer, High Moor (North Yorkshire), 2014 mixed media on paper 68 x 86 cms 26¾ x 33⅞ ins Yorkshire

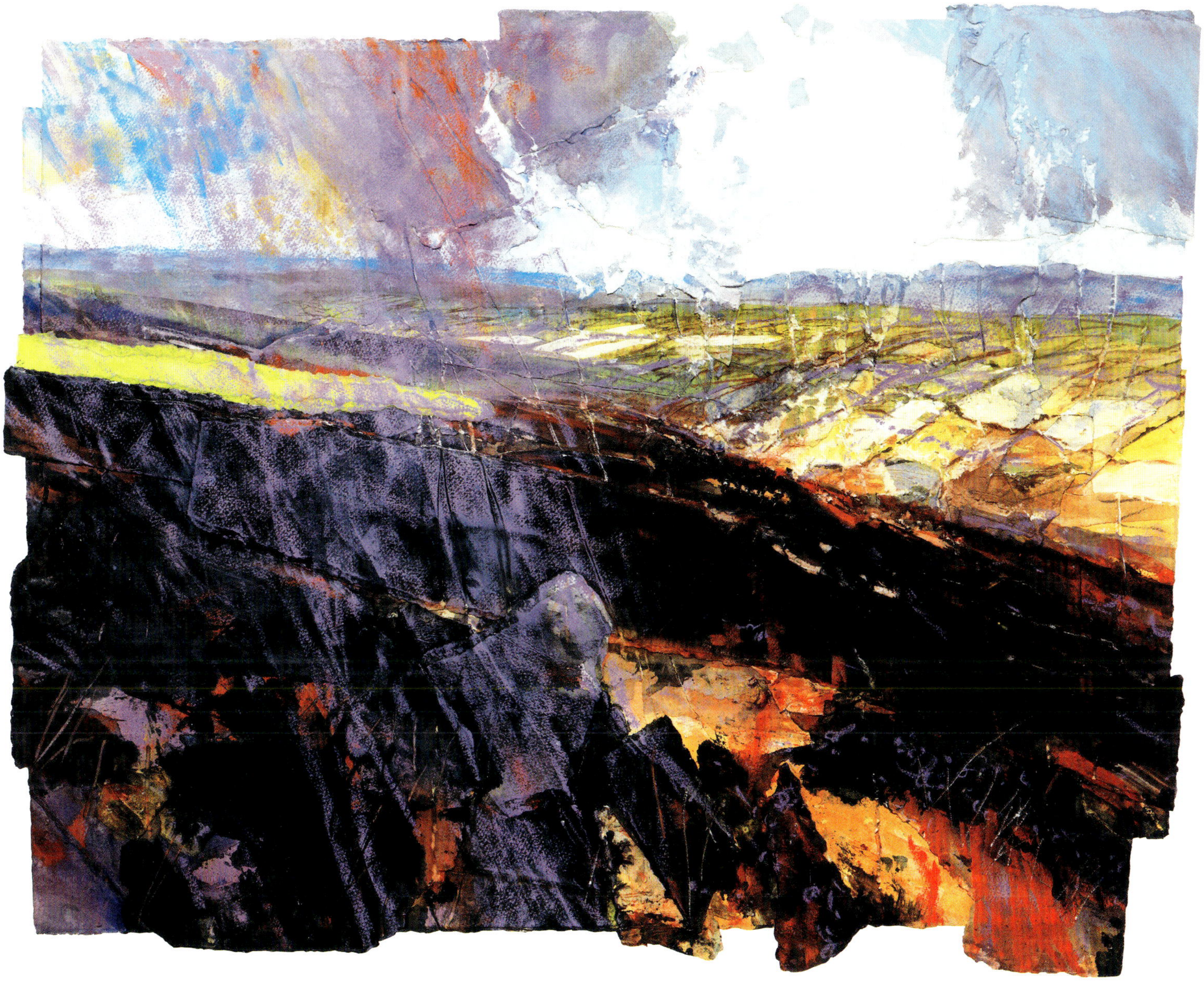

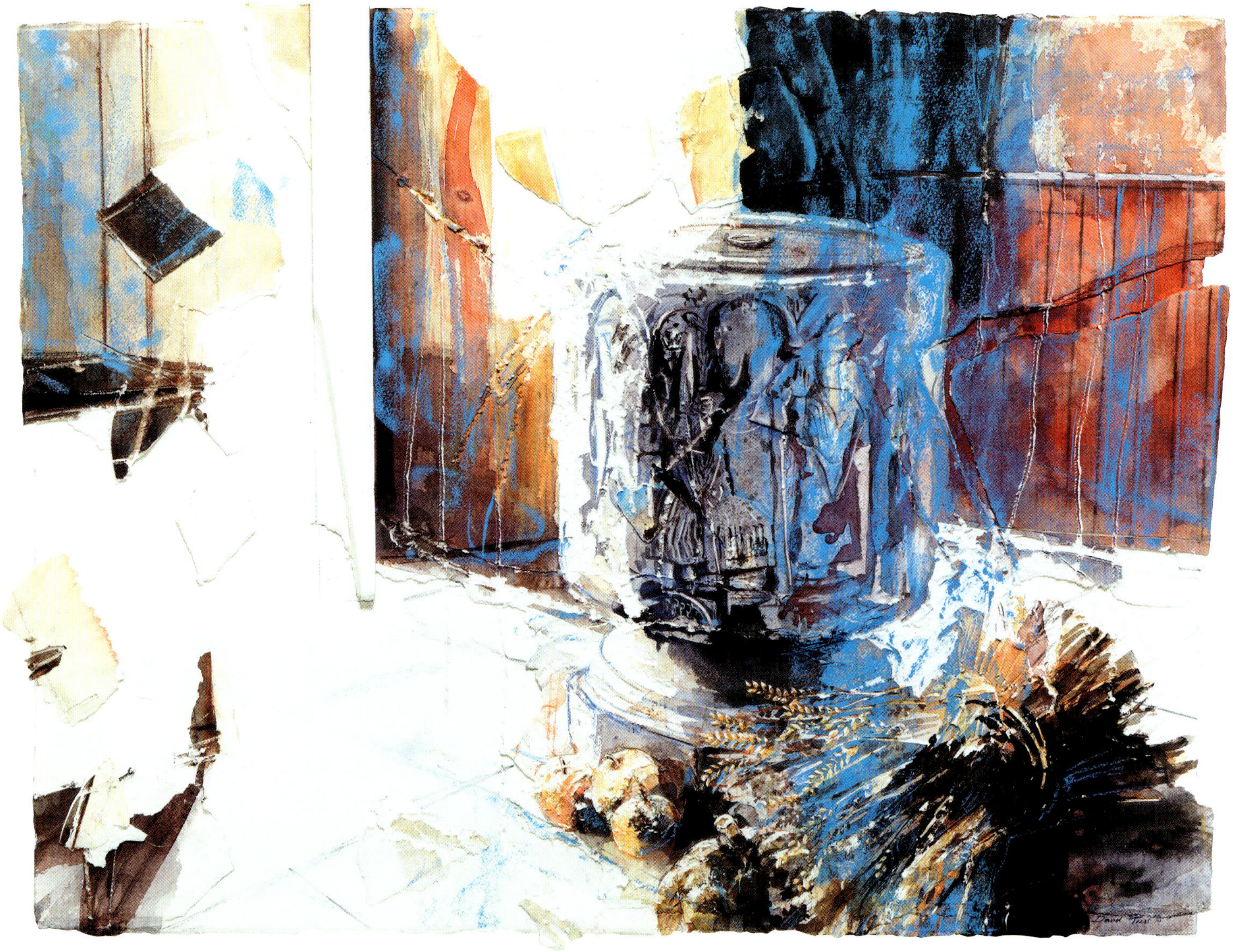

38 Light, Cowlam (North Yorkshire), 2014 mixed media on paper 61 x 80 cms 24 x 31½ ins Yorkshire

39 Light, North Grimston (North Yorkshire), 2014 mixed media on paper 78 x 62 cms 30¾ x 24⅜ ins Yorkshire

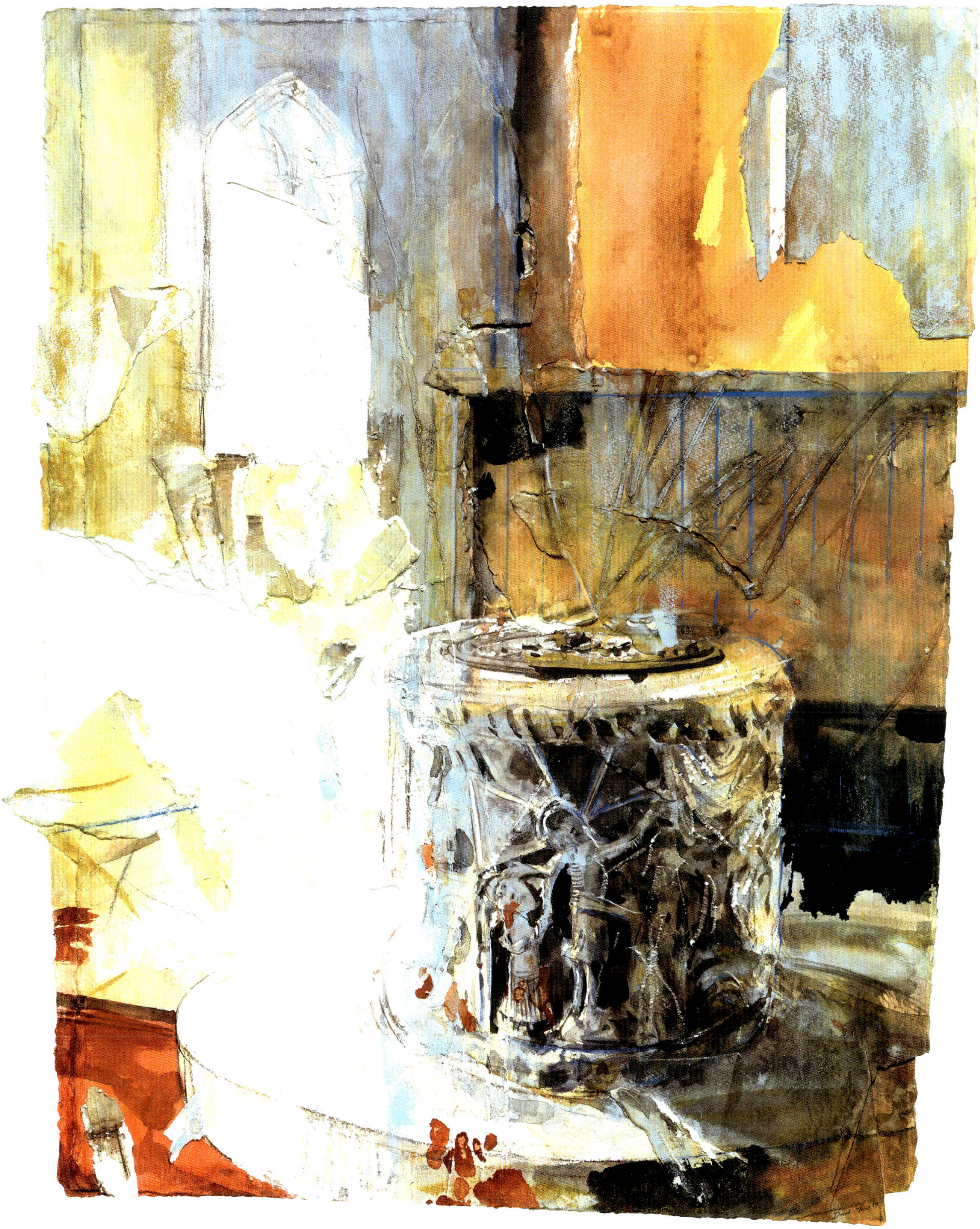

40 Summer, North Yorkshire (Above Clapham), 2014 mixed media on paper 66 x 93 cms 26 x 36⅝ ins Yorkshire

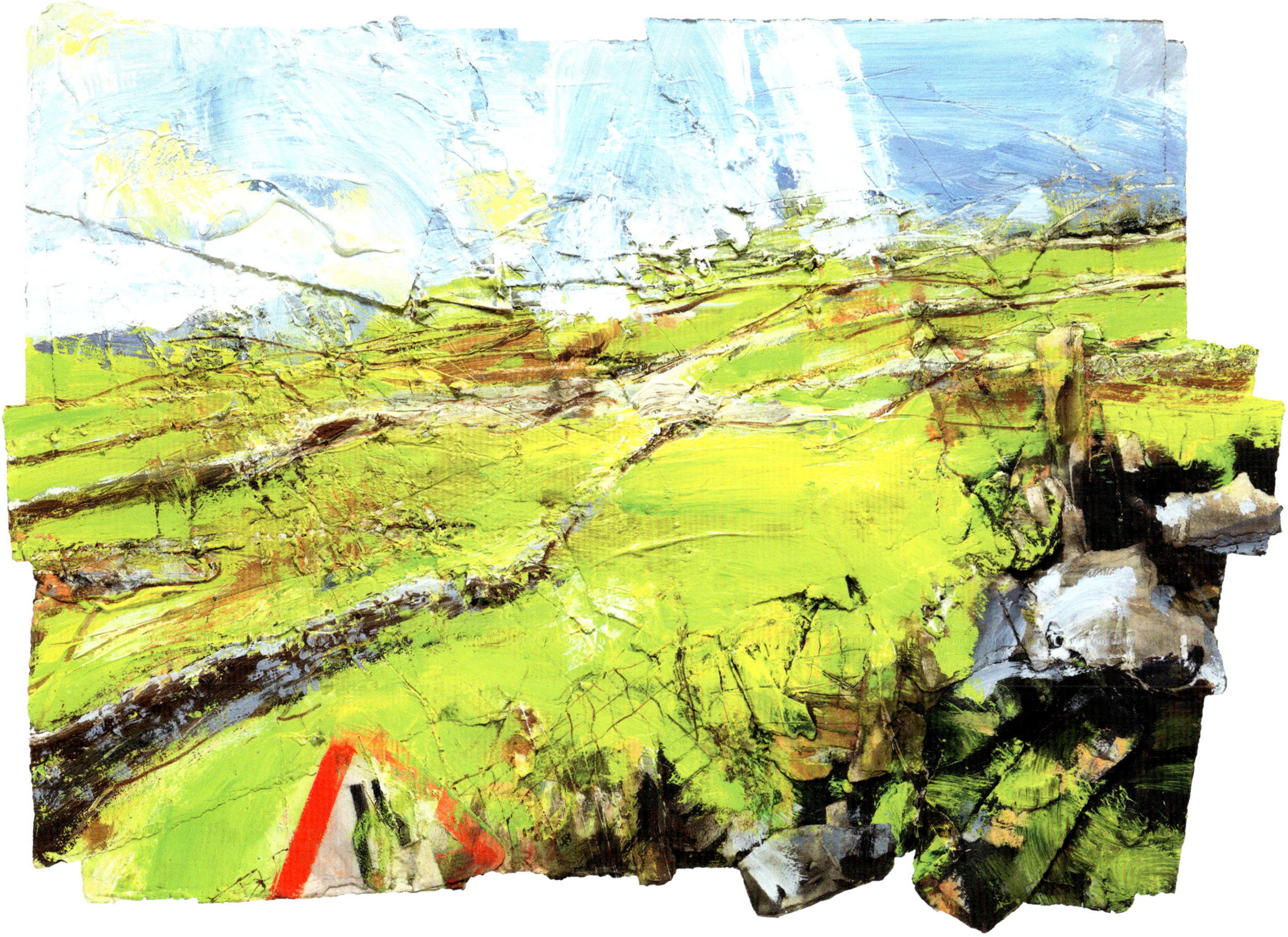

41 Big Gorse and Ingleborough, 2014 mixed media on paper 66 x 91 cms 26 x 35⅞ ins Yorkshire

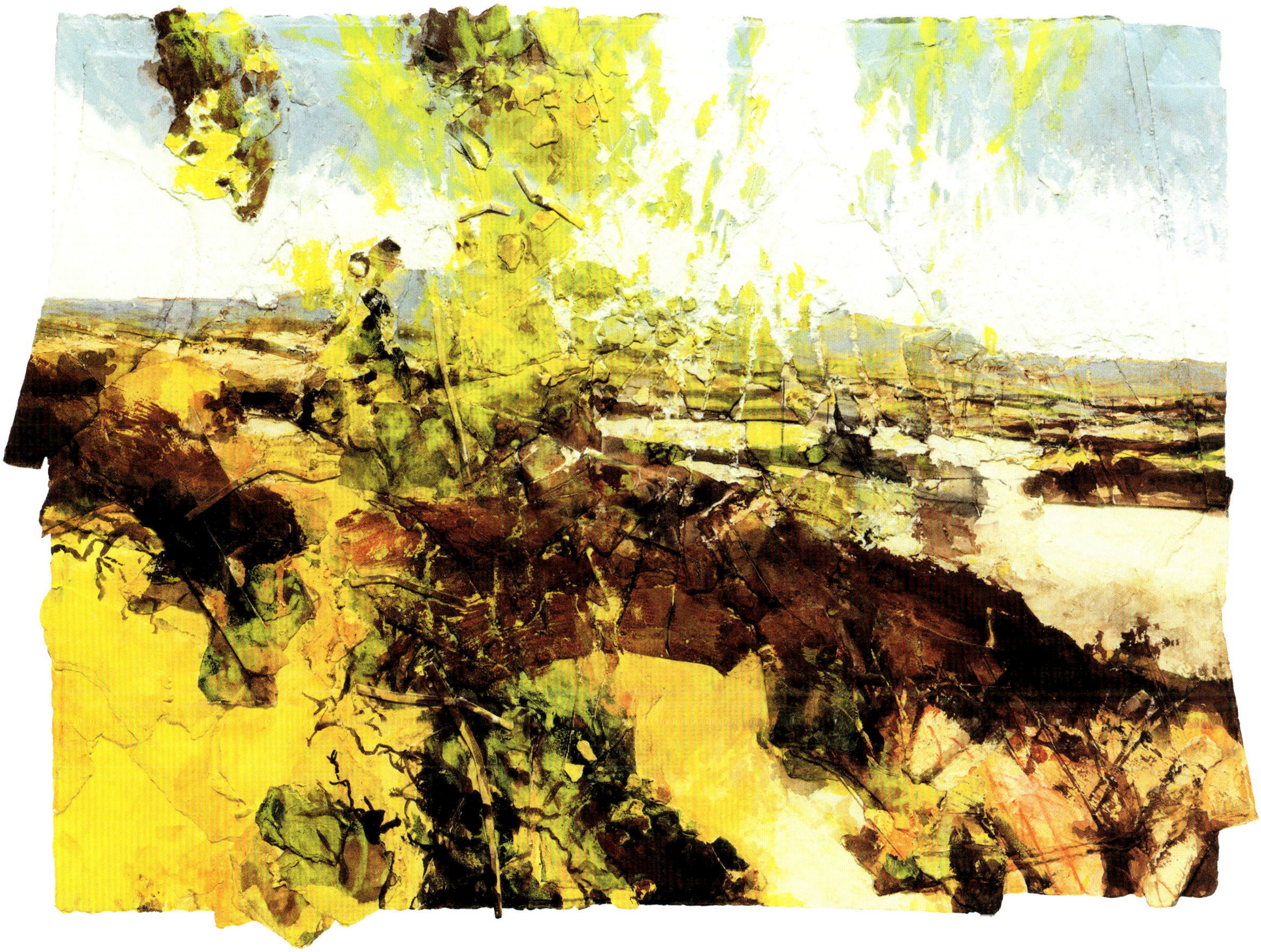

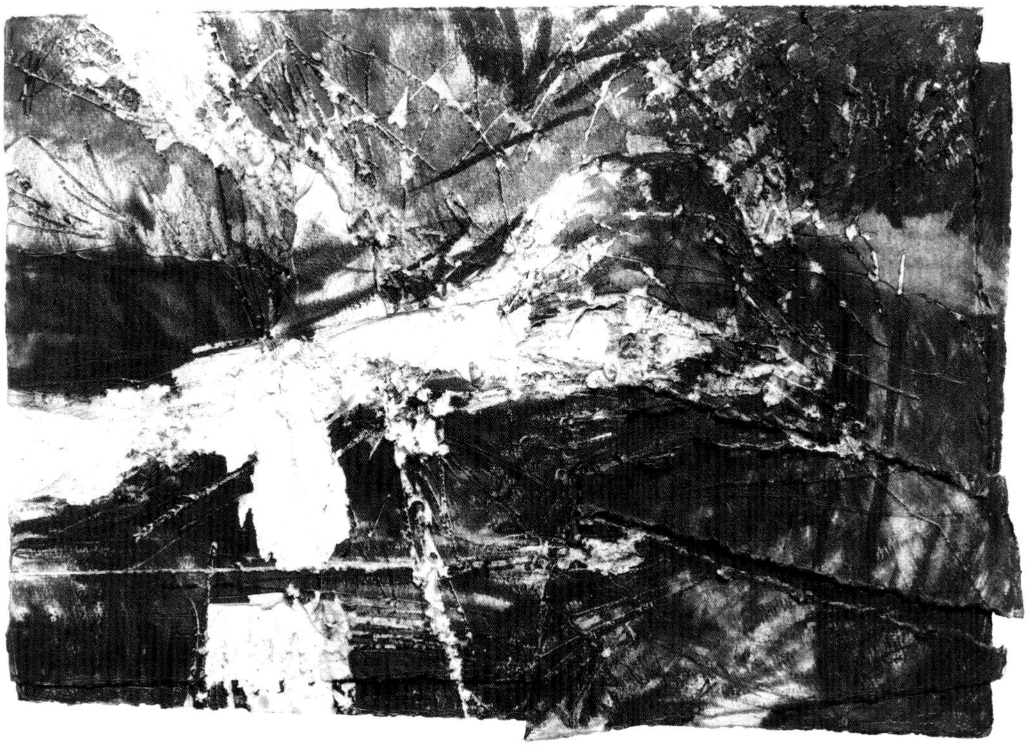

42 Burst of Light Beinn Bhan, 2009 graphite on paper 42 x 59 cms 16½ x 23¼ ins Scotland
43 Light Suddenly, Beinn Bhan, 2014 mixed media on paper 52 x 80 cms 20½ x 31½ ins Scotland

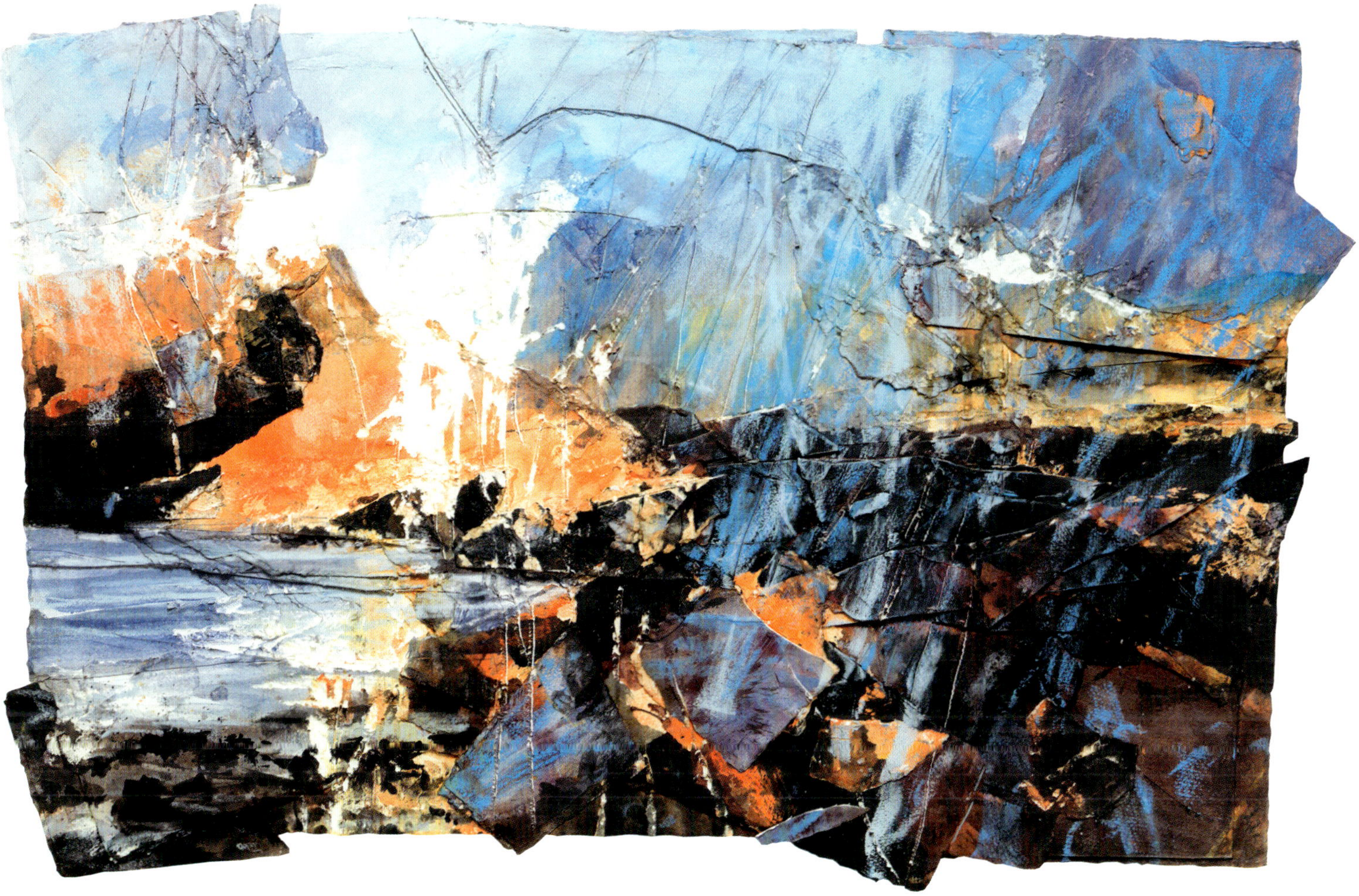

44 Sun Passing, Loch Torridon (Rainbow), 2014 mixed media on paper 32 x 40 cms 12⅝ x 15¾ ins Scotland

45 The Cuillins From Ard Dubh, 2014 mixed media on paper 32 x 40 cms 12⅝ x 15¾ ins Scotland

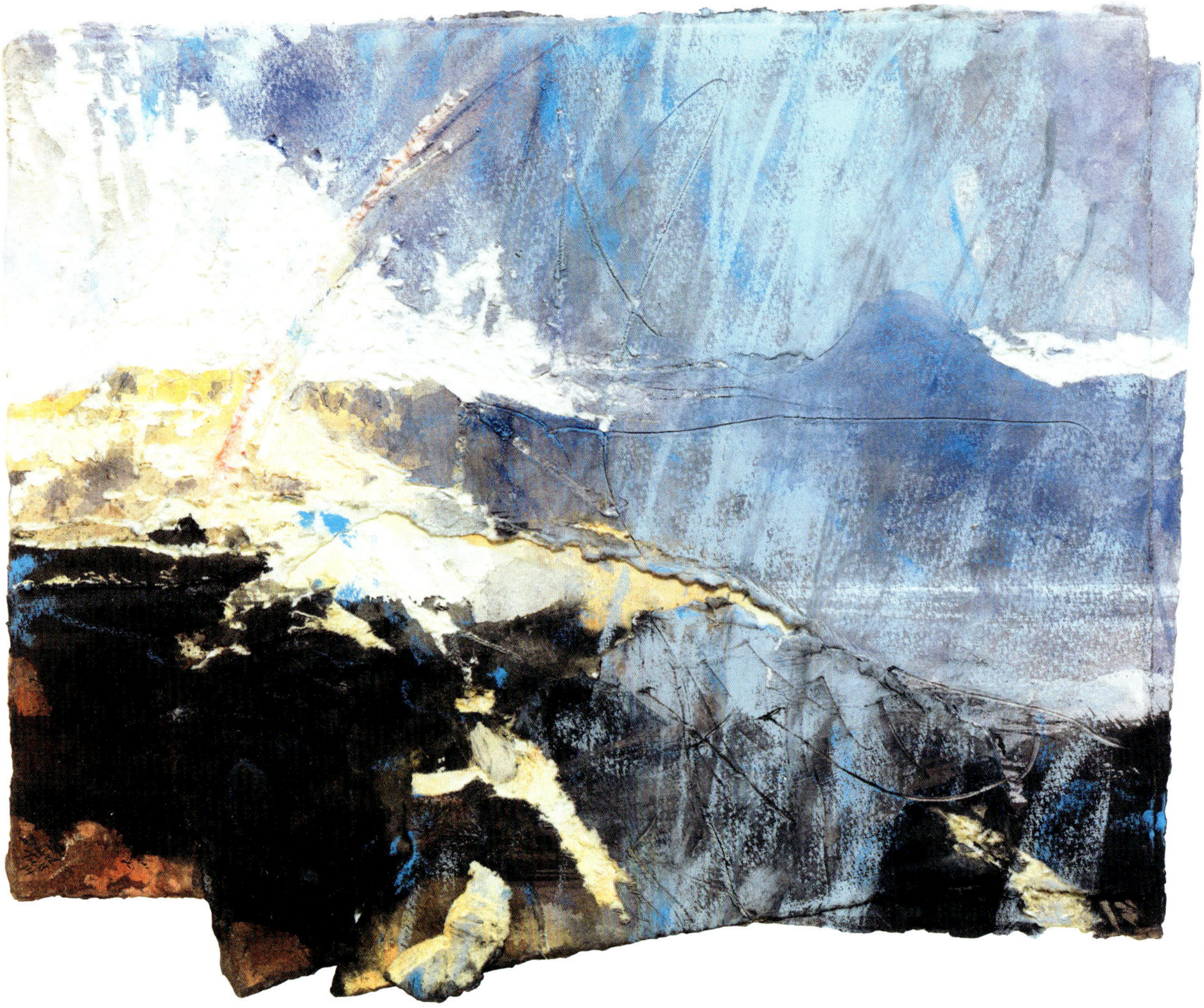

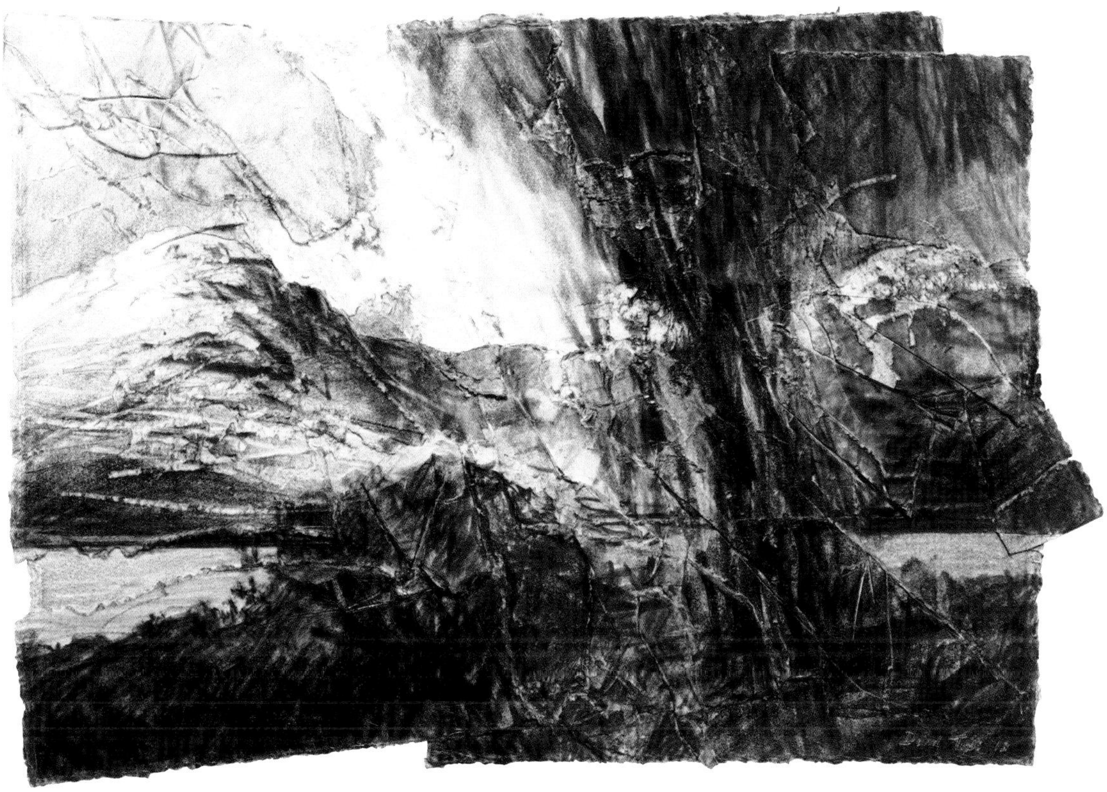

46 Snow, Beinn Bhan, 2013 graphite on paper 44 x 66 cms 17⅜ x 26 ins Scotland

47 Big Sun Suddenly, Ben Damph, 2012 mixed media on paper 46 x 70 cms 18⅛ x 27½ ins Scotland

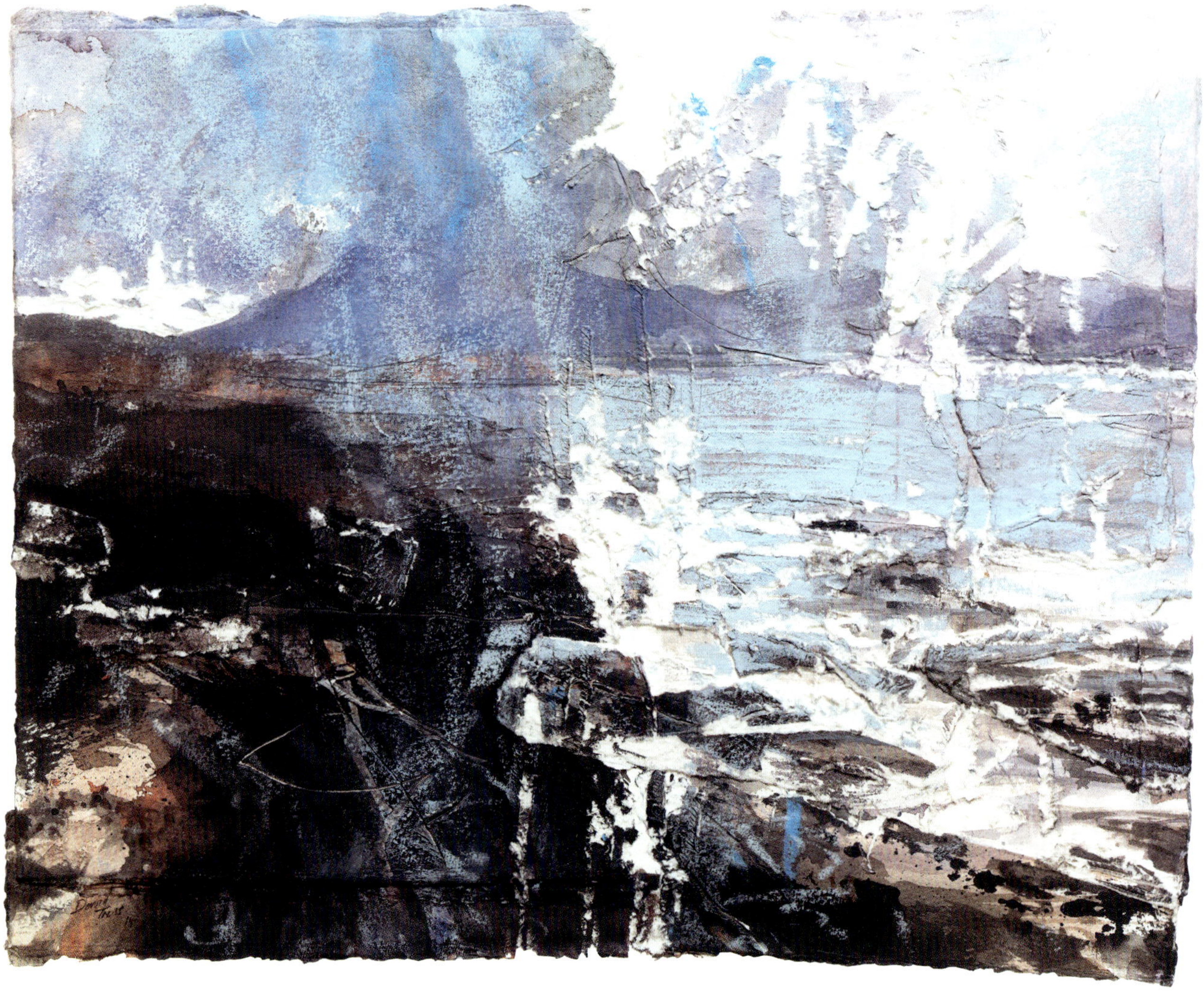

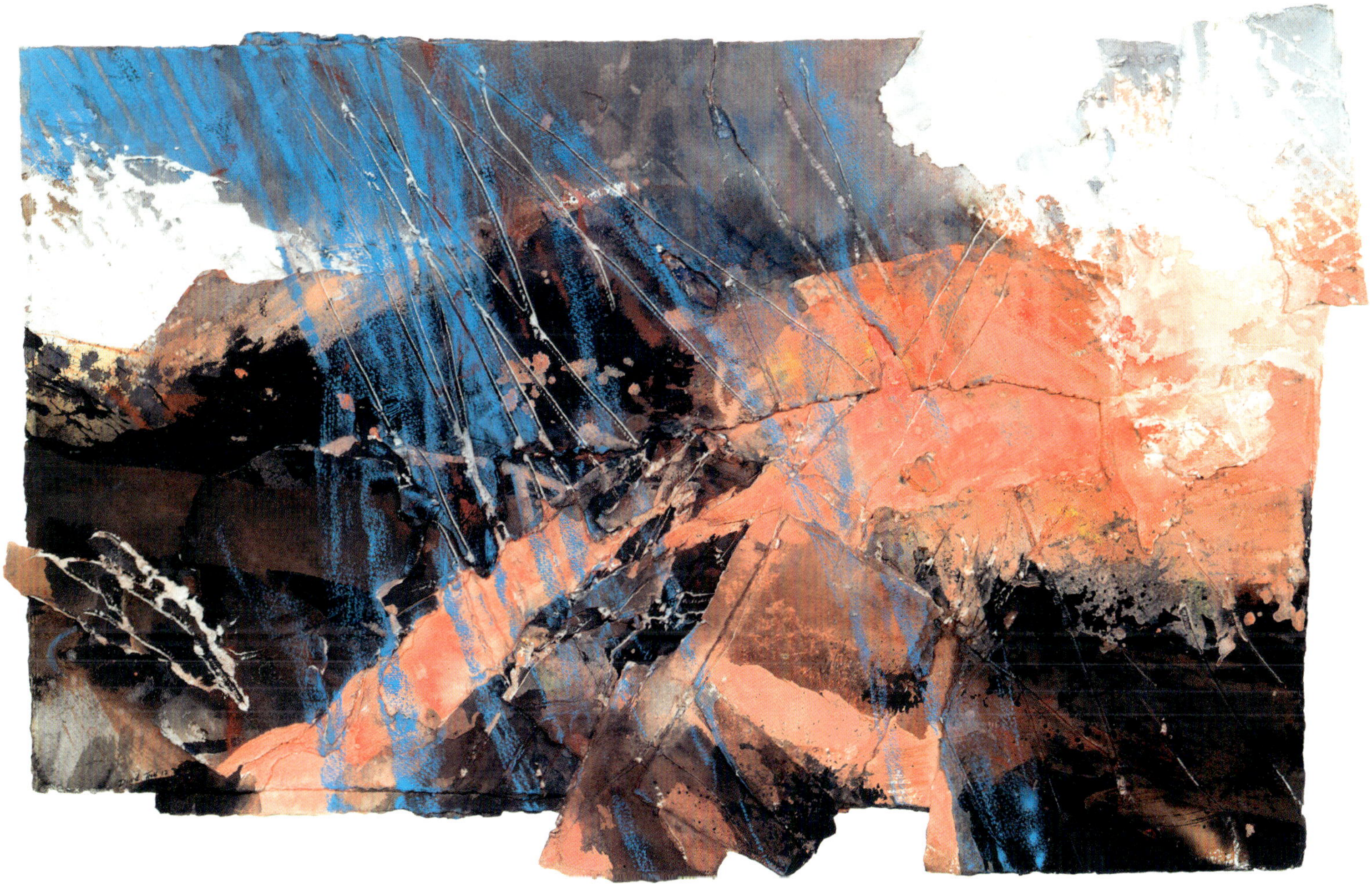

48 Light at Ard Dubh, 2014 mixed media on paper 33 x 40 cms 13 x 15¾ ins Scotland

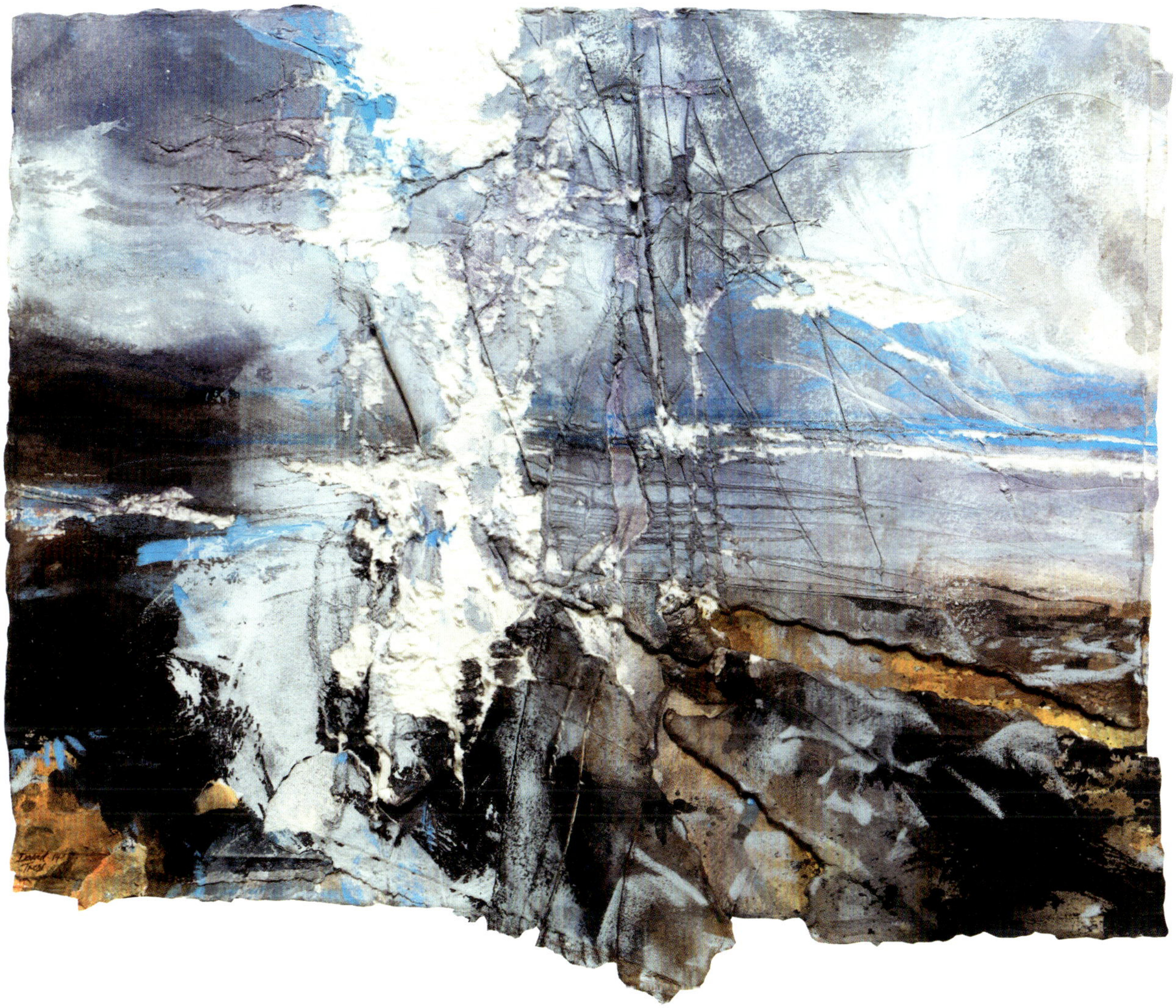

49 Looking, Loch Loin (Passing Sun), 2014 mixed media on paper 31 x 42 cms 12¼ x 16½ ins Scotland

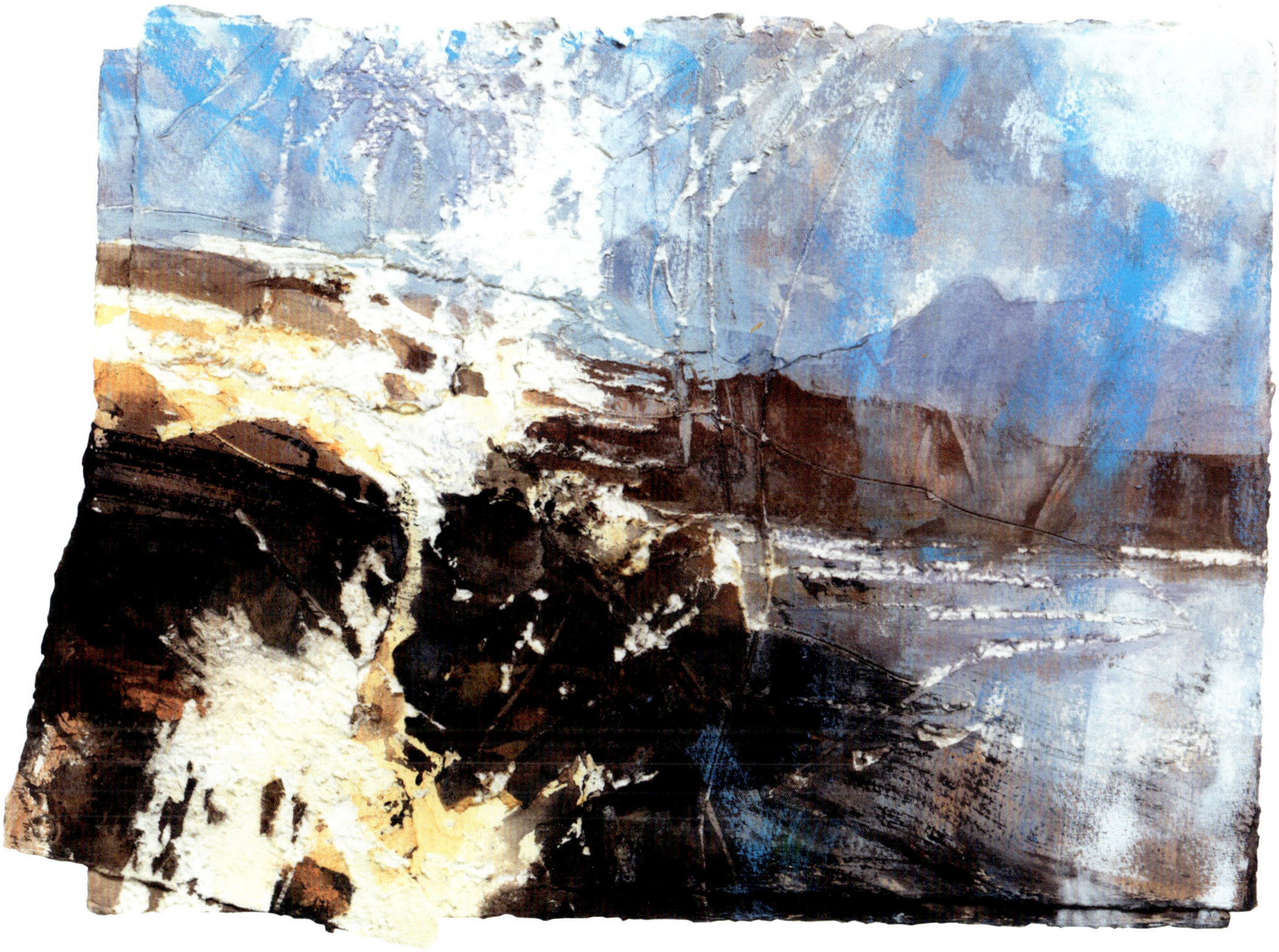

50 Sudden Sun, Meall Gorm, 2014 mixed media on paper 32 x 42 cms $12\frac{5}{8}$ x $16\frac{1}{2}$ ins Scotland

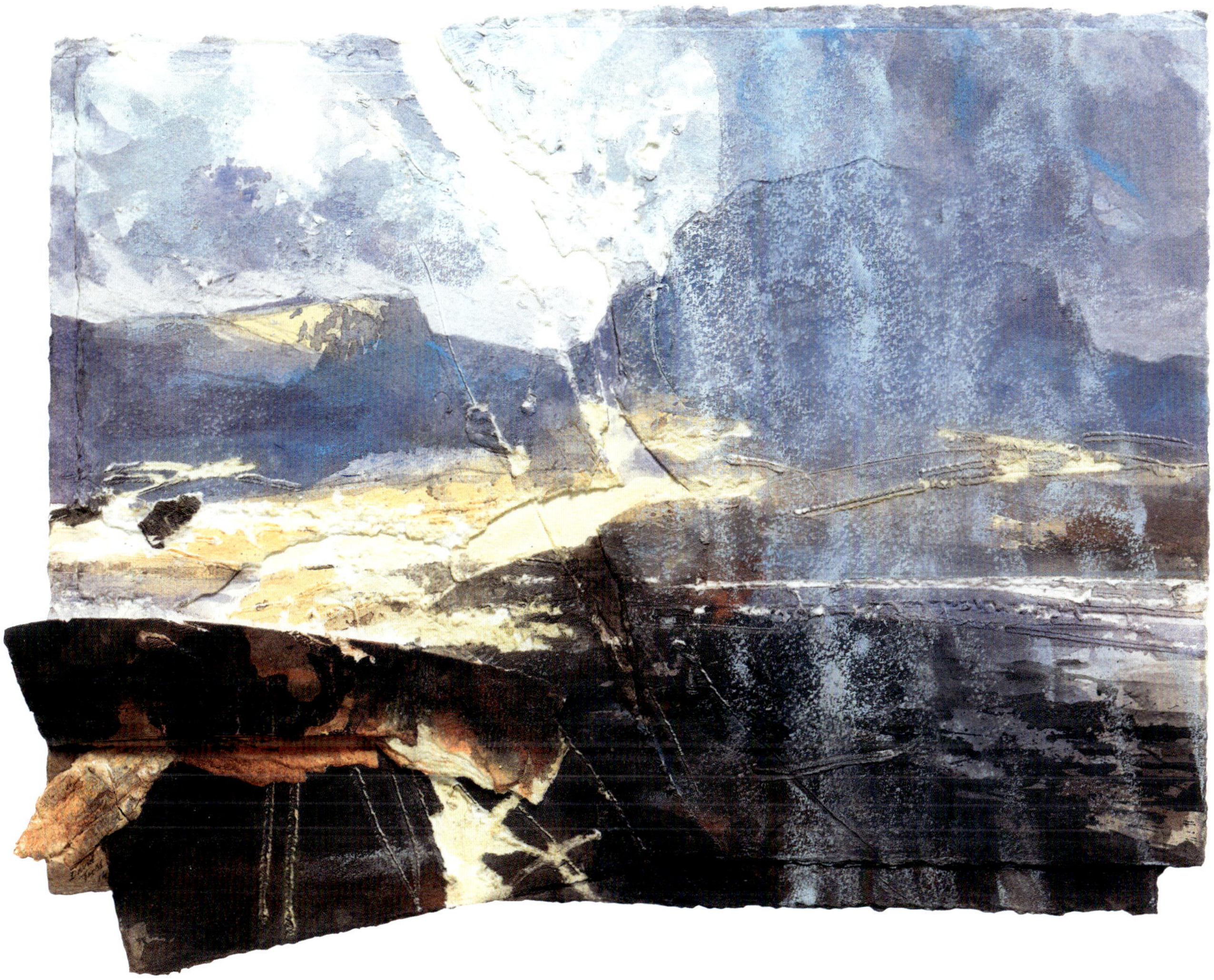

51 Shower and Sudden Light (Lower Loch Torridon), 2014 mixed media on paper 31 x 40 cms 12¼ x 15¾ ins Scotland

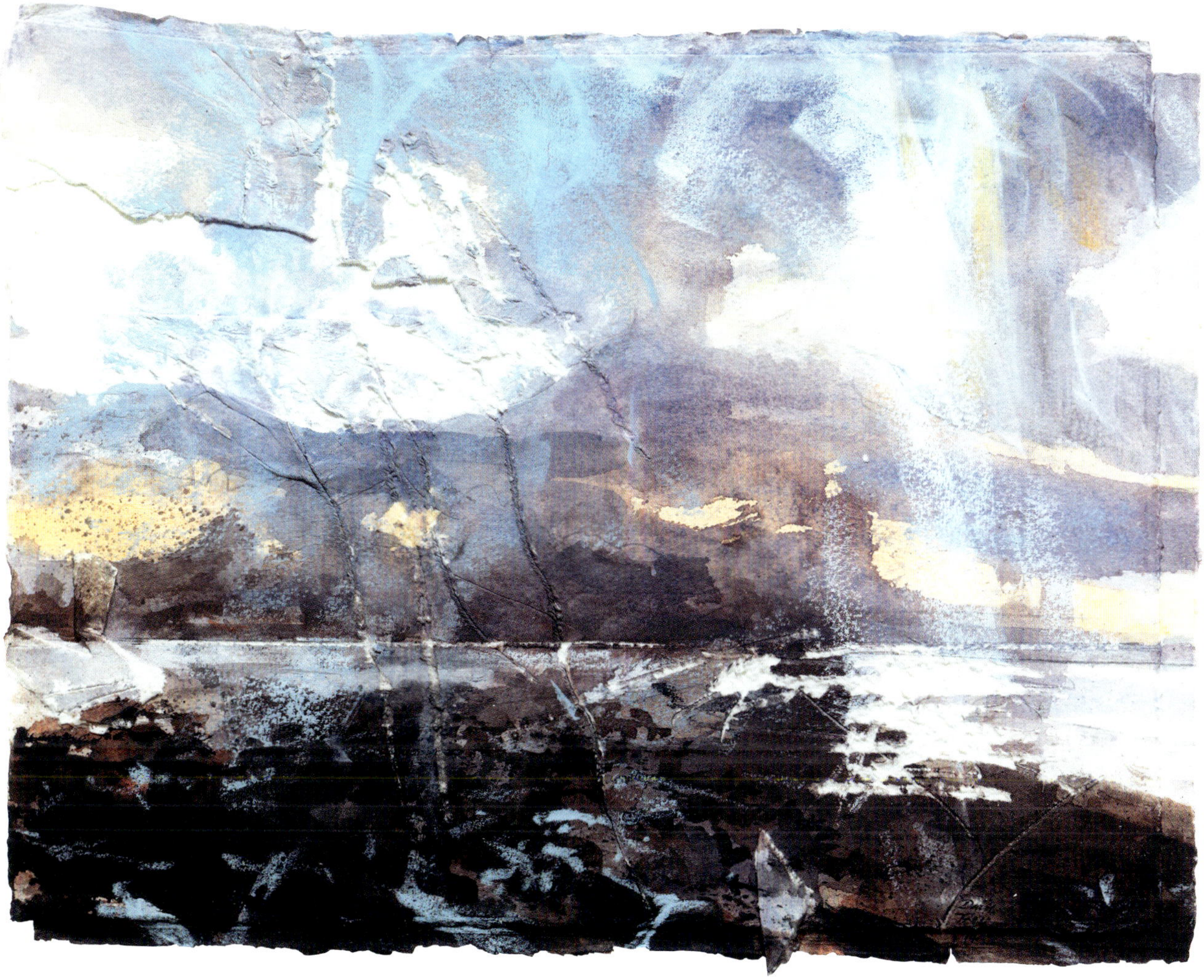

52 Rainbow, Loch Torridon, 2014 mixed media on paper 34 x 42 cms 13⅜ x 16½ ins Scotland

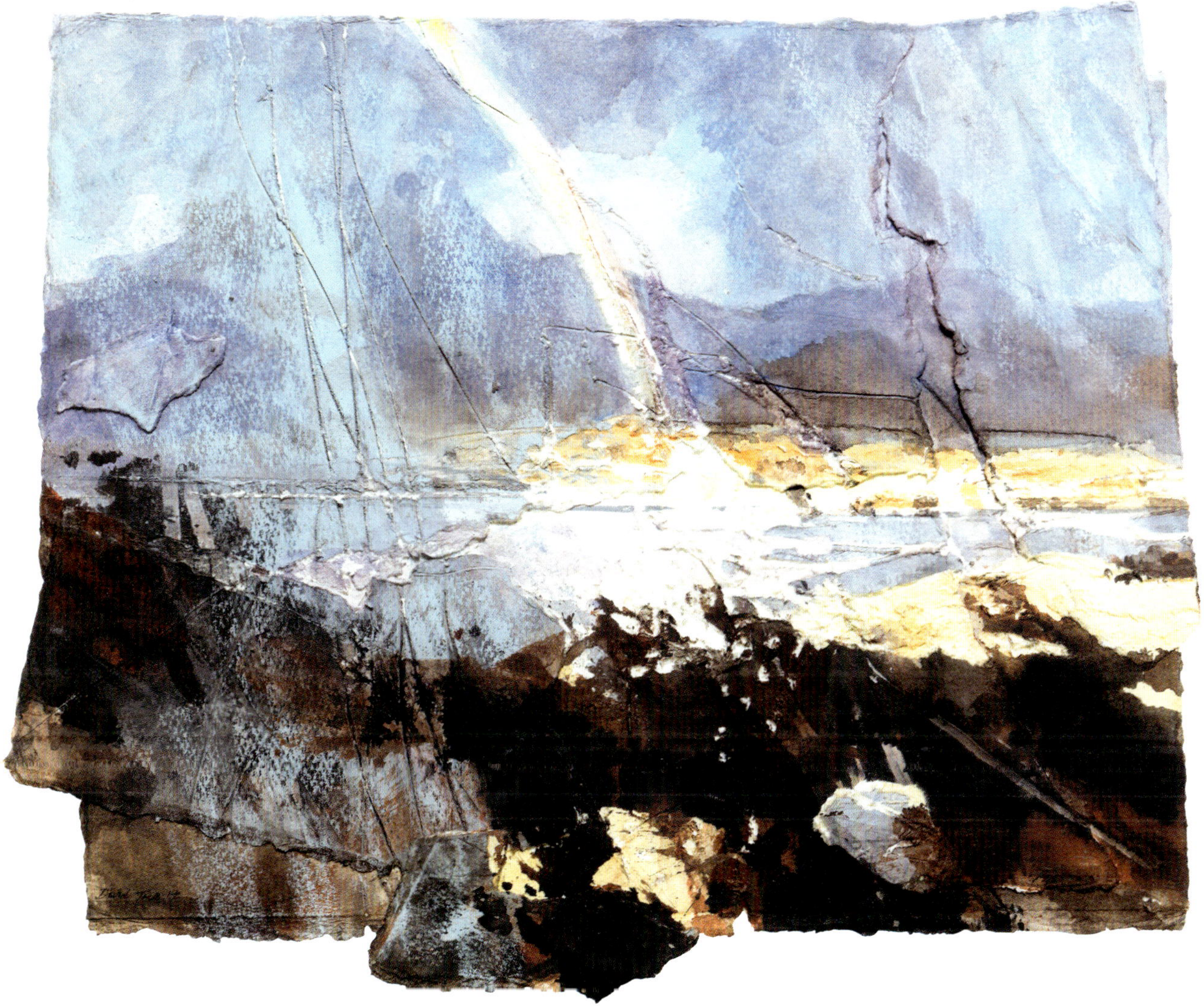

53 Low Tide, Camusterrach (Seeing Skye), 2014 mixed media on paper 49 x 64 cms 19¼ x 25¼ ins Scotland

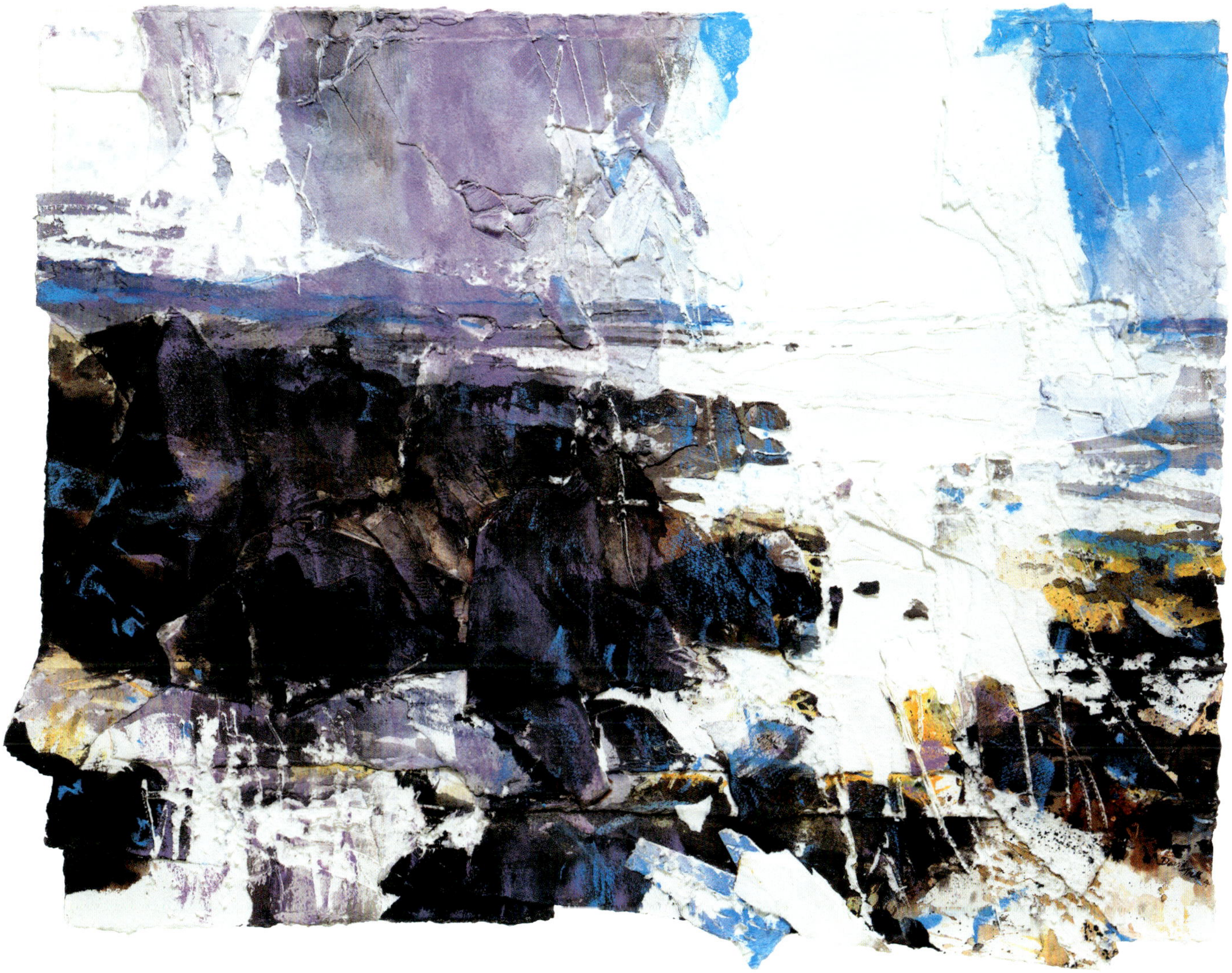

54 Sun on Aligin, 2014 mixed media on paper 51 x 76 cms 20⅛ x 29⅞ ins Scotland

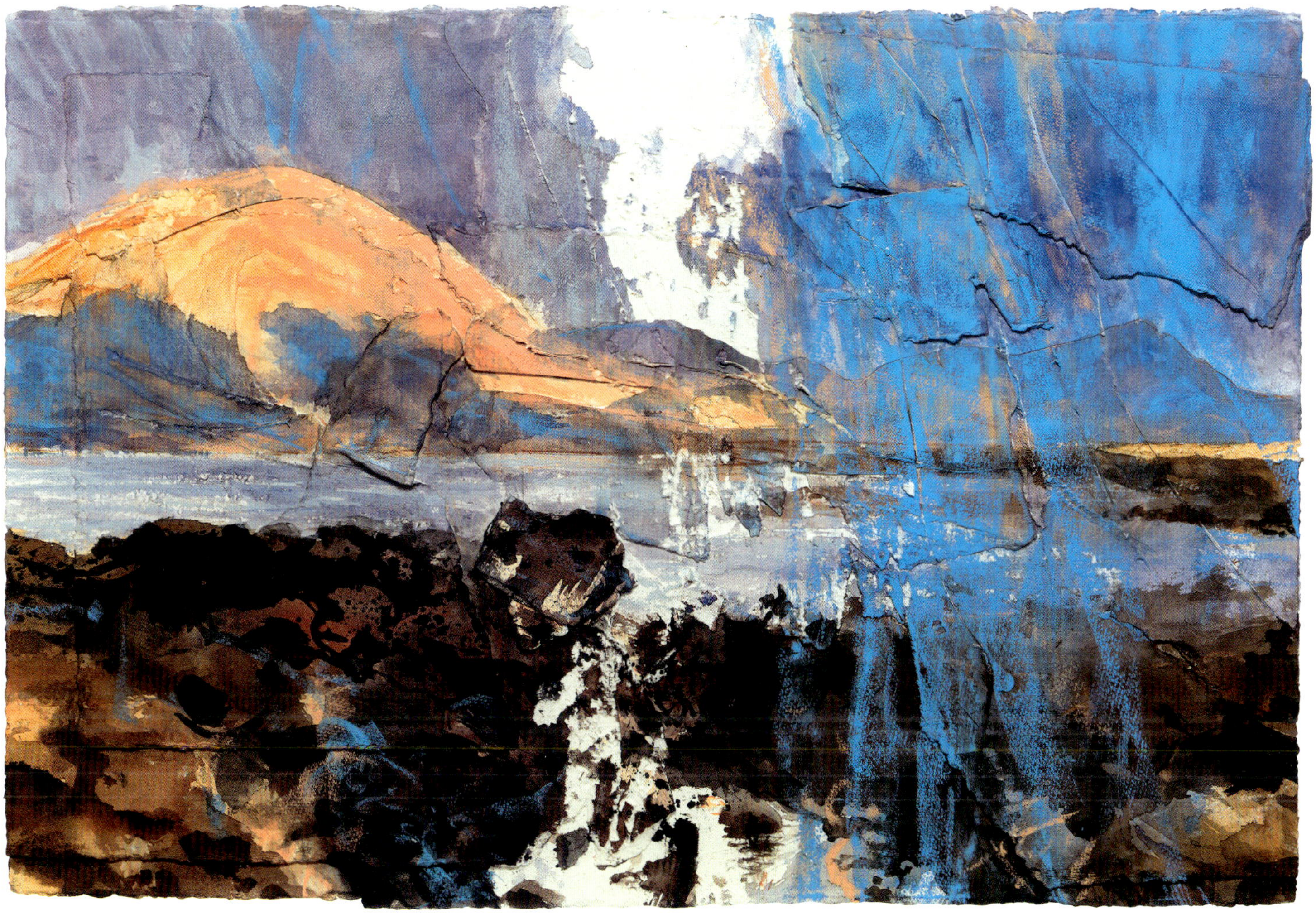

55 Cloud Lifting From Meall Gorm, 2013 mixed media on paper 56 x 74 cms 22 x 29⅛ ins Scotland

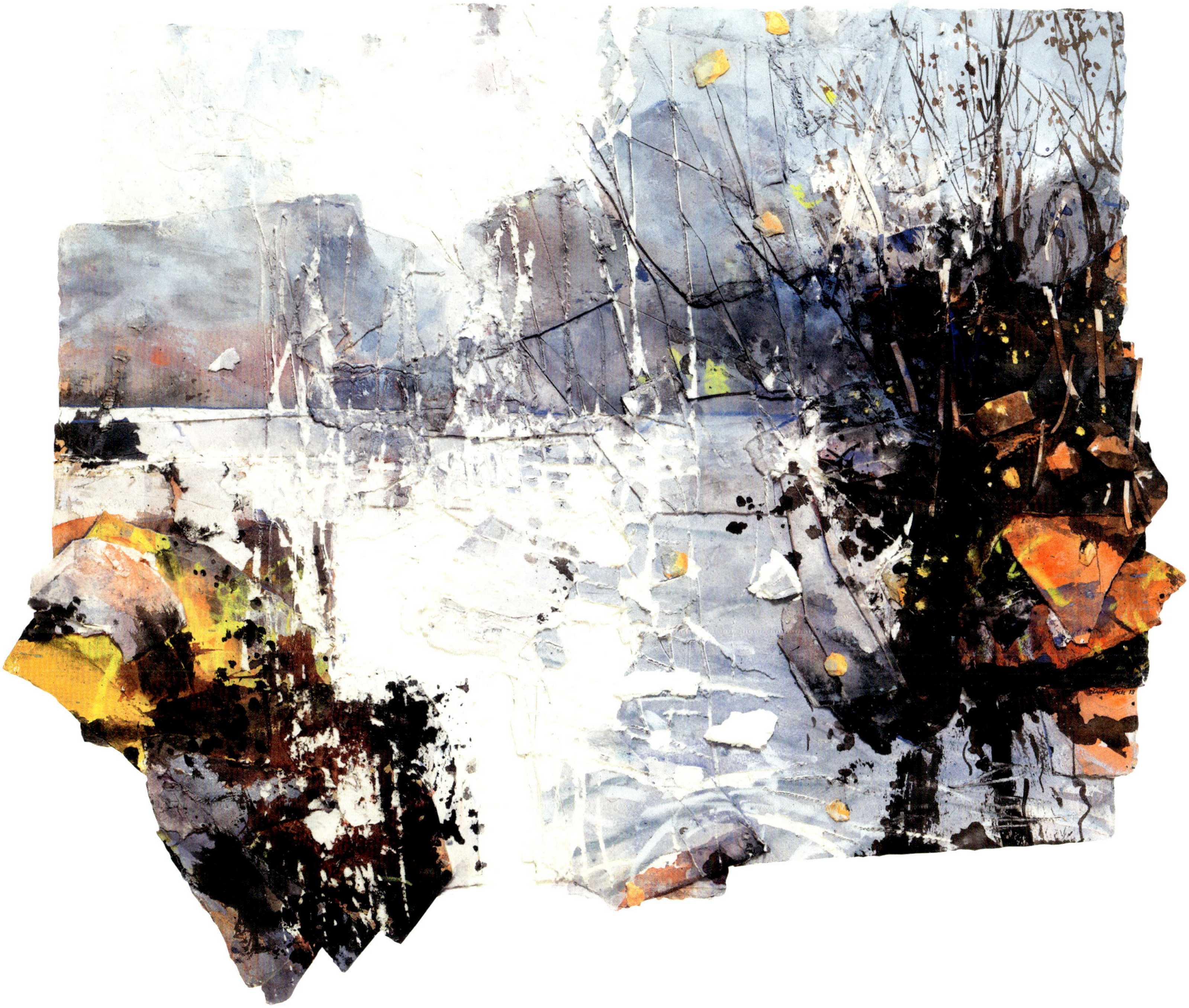

56 Rain over the Loch, 2013 mixed media on paper 51 x 75 cms 20⅛ x 29½ ins Scotland

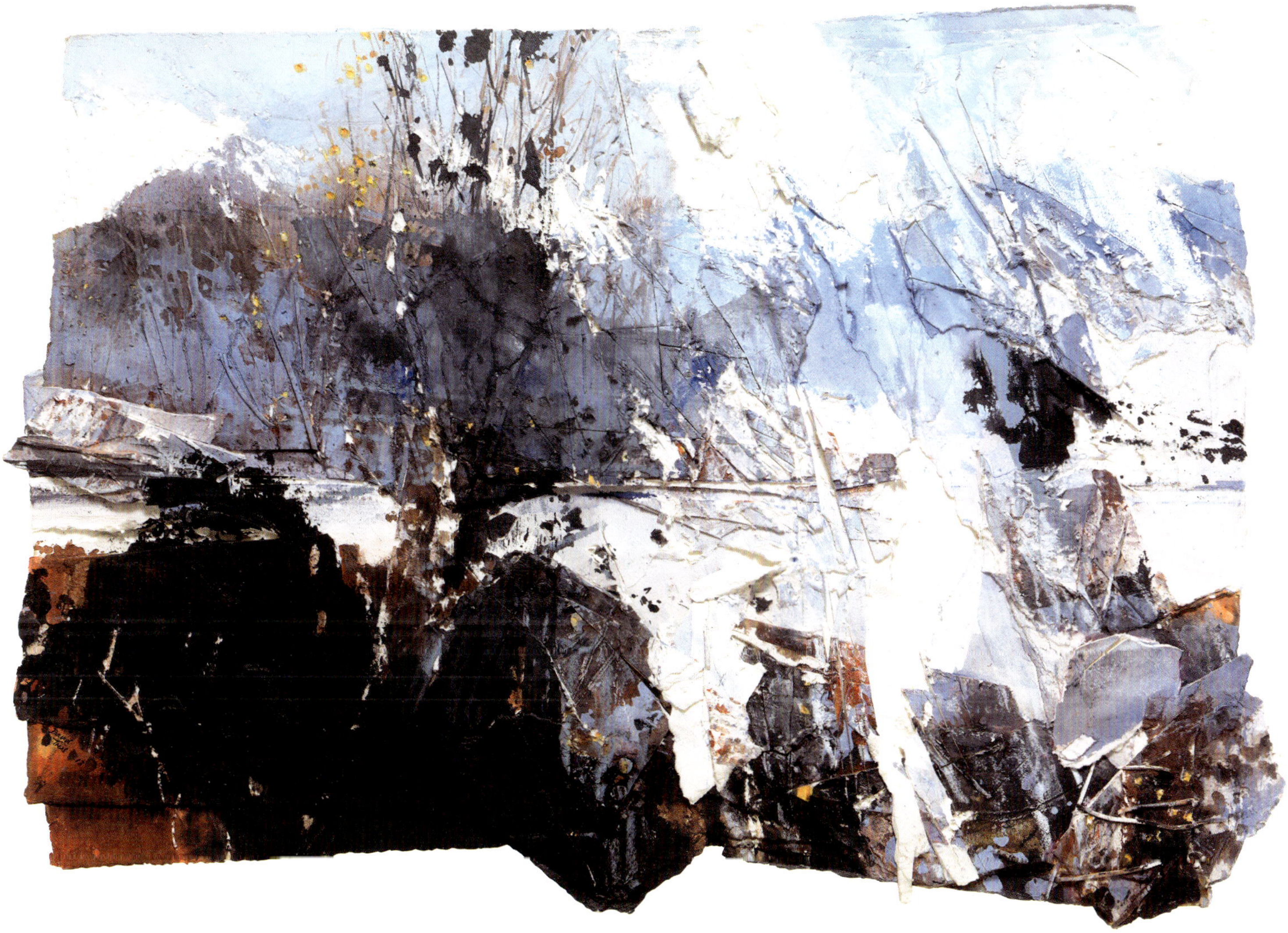

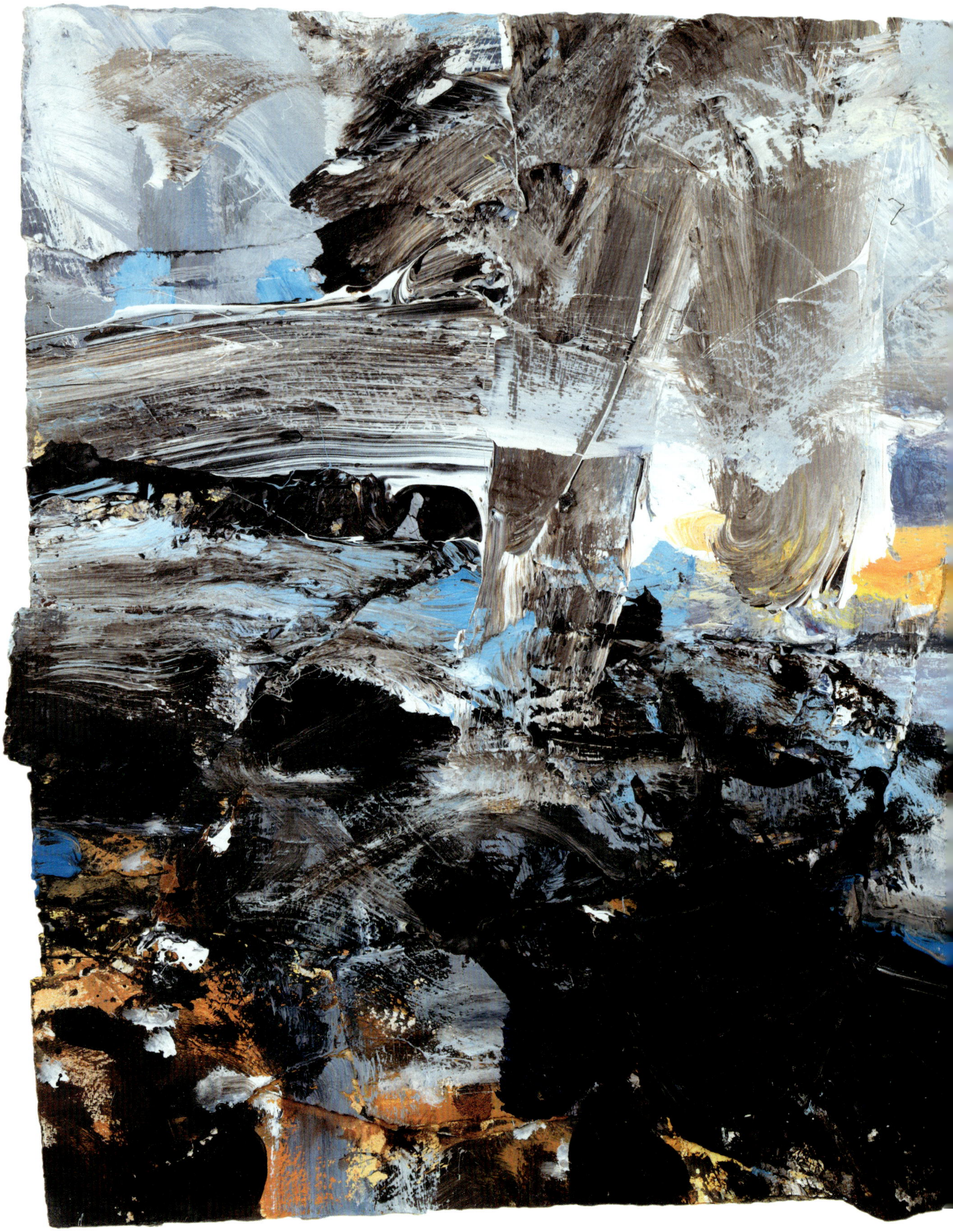

57 Aligin Appears (Loch Torridon), 2013 mixed media on paper 59 x 102 cms 23¼ x 40⅛ ins Scotland

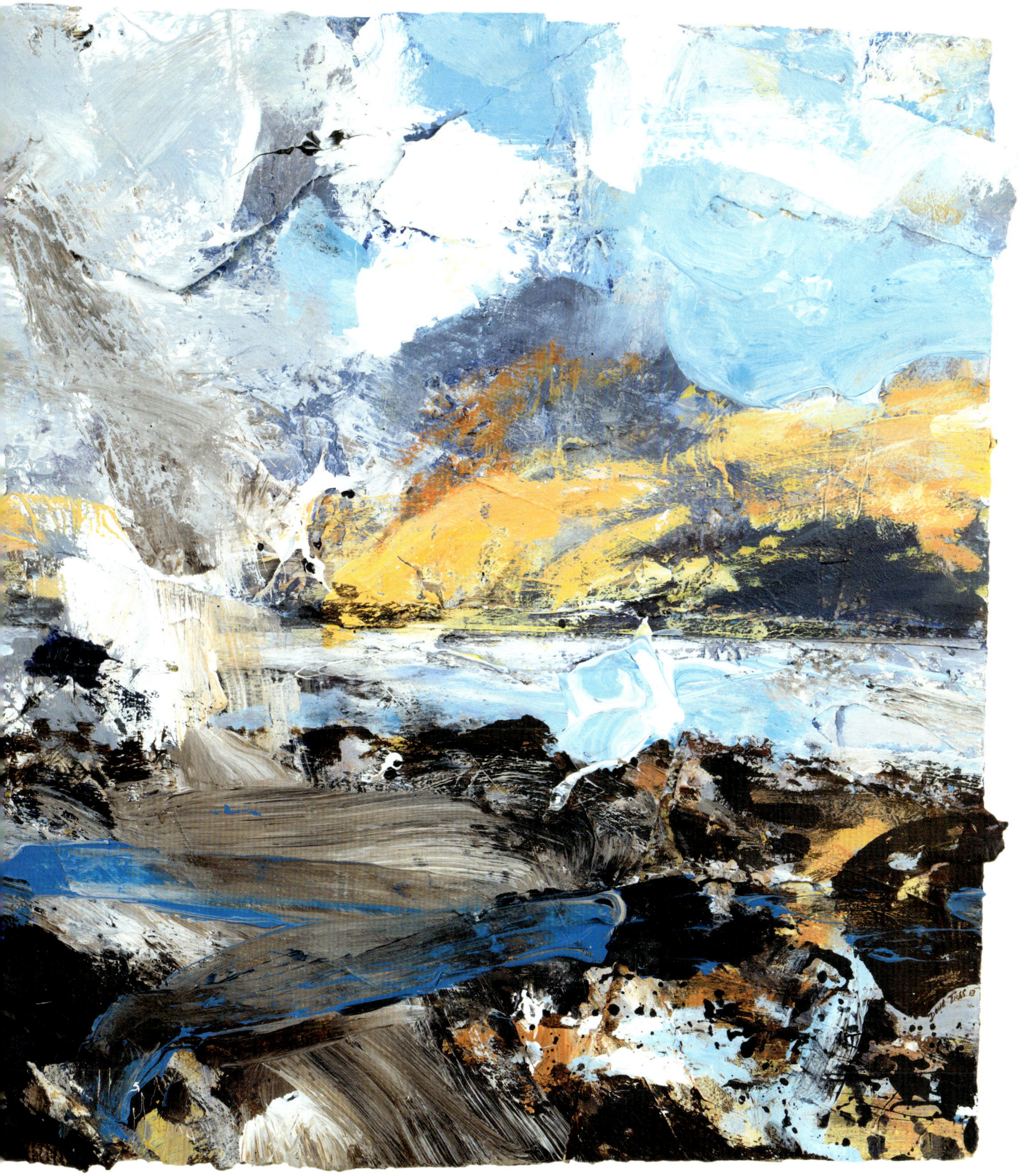

DAVID TRESS

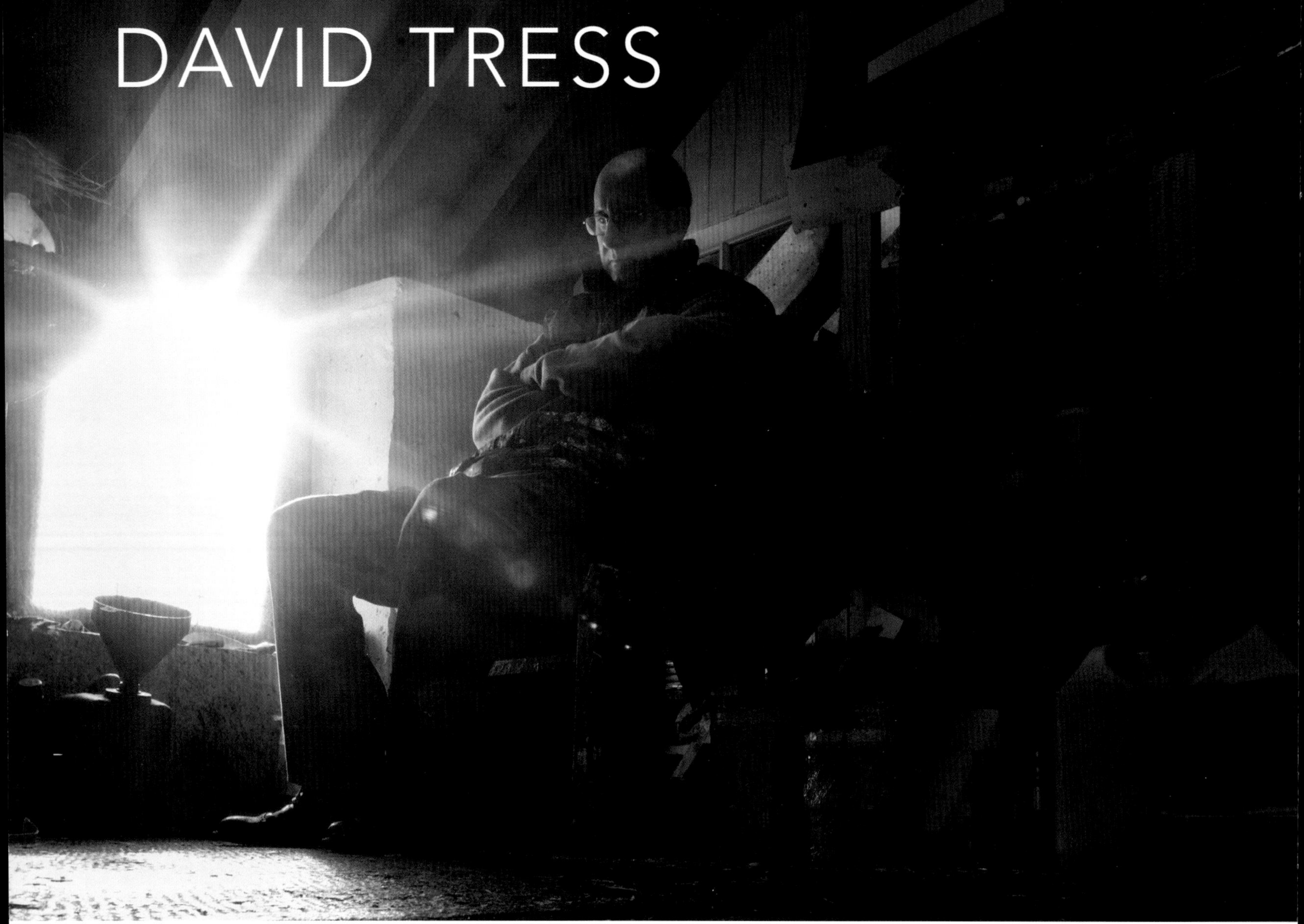

BIOGRAPHY

1955	Born London, Harrow College of Art Trent Polytechnic
1976	Moved to Wales, Taught History of Art at the University College of Wales, Aberystwyth

SOLO EXHIBITIONS

1982	Torch Theatre Gallery, Milford Haven
1987, 1990	Pauline Harries Gallery, Newport, Pembrokeshire
1988, 92, 99, 2001	Oriel Plas Glyn-y-Weddw, Llanbedrog, Gwynedd
1991, 94, 2000, 02, 2004, 06, 08, 10	West Wales Arts Centre, Fishguard, Pembrokeshire
1992	Salon d'Automne, Albi, France
1993, 95, 99, 2001, 2003, 05, 07, 09	Albany Gallery, Cardiff
1994	Taliesin Arts Centre, University of Swansea
1995, 98, 2001, 2003, 05, 07, 09, 11	Boundary Gallery, London
1997	Travelling exhibition commencing West Wales Arts Centre, Fishguard then to Royal Cambrian Academy, Conwy and Albany Gallery, Cardiff
2001	Glynn Vivian Art Gallery, Swansea
2003	Museum of Modern Art, Wales
2003–05	'David Tress. Drawings'. Travelling exhibition commencing Brecknock Museum and Art Gallery, Brecon; then to Newport Museum and Art Gallery, Newport, South Wales; Midlands Arts Centre, Birmingham; National Library of Wales, Aberystwyth; Guildhall Art Gallery, London; West Wales Arts Centre, Fishguard

2005	Denbighshire Arts. Travelling Exhibition
2005/07	Brian Sinfield Gallery, Burford
2006	Clwyd Theatr Cymru, Mold, Flintshire
2008–11	'Chasing Sublime Light'. Travelling exhibition commencing MOMA Wales, then to Petworth House, West Sussex; Clwyd Theatr Cymru, Mold; Gallery Oldham; Keswick Museum and Art Gallery; Worcester City Art Gallery and Museum; The National Library of Wales; Oriel Ynys Mon, Anglesey; West Wales Arts Centre, Fishguard; The Maclaurin Galleries, Ayr; Stowe School, Buckingham; Royal Cambrian Academy, Conwy.
2009, 11, 14	John Davies Gallery, Moreton-in-Marsh
2010	'Landmarks'. Victoria Art Gallery, Bath.
2011, 14	Beaux Arts, Bath
2012, 13, 15	Messum's, London

GROUP EXHIBITIONS

1980, 81	Oriel (Welsh Arts Council), Cardiff
1981, 82	Royal Society of British Artists
1983–2011	Albany Gallery, Cardiff
1984	'Pembrokeshire Artists', travelling exhibition organised by Pembrokeshire Museums
1984–2012	West Wales Arts Centre, Fishguard
1985–99	Pauline Harries Gallery, Newport, Pembrokeshire
1986	Fulham Gallery, London
1986–88	Pelter Sands Gallery, Bristol
1987–99, 2003	Attic Gallery, Swansea
1988–95	Oriel Plas Glyn-y-Weddw, Llanbedrog, Gwynedd
1990	Cadogan Contemporary, London/Trumpington Gallery, Cambridge
1990, 91	Nature Conservancy Council, travelling exhibition
1991	Vanessa Devereux Gallery, London
1993	Gallerie Lughien, Amsterdam
1993	Five Artists From Wales, Eleonore Austerer Gallery, San Francisco
1995–2011	Boundary Gallery, London
1998	Invited artist, Eigse Carlow Arts Festival, Republic of Ireland,
1998	'Landmarks', National Museum Wales, Cardiff
1999	'Mountain', Wolverhampton Art Gallery
2000	Garter Lane Arts Centre, Waterford, Republic of Ireland
2001	Museum of Modern Art, Wales
2002	Beaux Arts, Bath
2003	Hereford City Art Gallery
2003, 05	'The Discerning Eye', London
2004	'Farming and the Welsh Landscape', travelling exhibition organised for the centenary of the Royal Welsh Agricultural Society
2005	'Tir Lun. Drawing', Oriel Myrddin Gallery, Carmarthen
2005	'Approaches to Landscape', King's School, Worcester
2005	'A Winter Journey', Art Space Gallery, London
2006	Yvonne Arnaud Exhibition, Guildford
2006	'Different Worlds', Brian Sinfield Gallery, Burford
2006	Twentieth Anniversary Exhibition, Boundary Gallery, London
2006	'Landscapes of Wales', National Botanic Garden of Wales
2006	'Critic's Choice' an exhibition selected by Andrew Lambirth including work by Craigie Aitchison, Gillian Ayres, Jeffery Camp, John Craxton, Robert Dukes, Maggi Hambling, Julian Perry, Cherry Pickles, George Rowlett, Ian Welsh, Jo Welsh. The Art Shop, Abergavenny
2008	'A Passion for Art', The Friends of the Glynn Vivian Art Gallery 50th Anniversary Exhibition
2008	Beaux Arts, Bath
2008	John Davies Gallery, Moreton-in-Marsh
2008	Pallant House Gallery, Chichester
2009	'Art Cymru: Modern Art in Wales', Pallant House Gallery, Chichester.
2009	The Art Shop, Abergavenny
2010	Beaux Arts, Bath
2010	John Davies Gallery, Moreton-in-Marsh
2010	'Retrospective'. Eigse Carlow Arts Festival, Ireland.
2011	Martin Tinney Gallery, Anglesey
2012	Messums, London
2012	Brian Sinfield Gallery, Burford. Fortieth Anniversary Exhibition

PRINCIPAL WORKS IN PUBLIC COLLECTIONS

(Alphabetical listing)
Brecknock Museum and Art Gallery
Ceredigion Museum
Clare Hall, Cambridge
The Contemporary Art Society for Wales
Dyfed County Council, County Hall Collection (now Carmarthenshire County Council)
The Glynn Vivian Art Gallery
The Guildhall Art Gallery, City of London
The Museum of Modern Art, Wales
The National Library of Wales
National Museums and Galleries of Wales
Pallant House Gallery
Pembrokeshire Museums

COMMISSIONS

In 2014 David Tress was commissioned by HRH The Prince of Wales to paint a picture of Llwynywermod, his house in Wales

Nature Conservancy Council

Development Board for Rural Wales, selector Peter Fuller

One of 48 British artists and designers commissioned by Royal Mail to design a stamp for the 1999 Millennium Stamp issue

Contemporary Art Society of Wales Anniversary Print Portfolio, 2008

Paintings reproduced on book covers :

'Frontiers in Anglo-Welsh Poetry' by Tony Conran, Cardiff, University of Wales Press, 1997

'Sacred Place, Chosen People' by Dorian Llewelyn, Cardiff, University of Wales Press, 1999

'Hen Dy Ffarm: The Old Farmhouse' by D J Williams, Trans. Waldo Williams, Llandysul, Gomer Press, 2001

'Voyaging Out' poems by Peter Abbs, Salt Publishing, 2009.

'Moor Music' by Mike Jenkins Seren, 2010

SELECTED REVIEWS

Daily Telegraph — 18 November 1972

Art Review — 11 and 25 August 1989, July 1991

La Depeche du Midi, France — 15 October 1992

Uned Gelf / The Art Unit — October 1992

Western Mail — 23 Sept 1995, 19 July 1997
Review: Rian Evans

Planet, The Welsh Internationalist — No 123 June/July1997
Review: Jill Piercy

Galleries — July 1997
Review: Clare Rendell

Modern Painters Vol 10, No 2 — Summer 1997
Review: Robert Macdonald

Irish Times — 11 June 1998
Review: Aidan Dunne

Western Mail — 2 Sept 1999
Review: Karen Price

Golwg — 16 Medi 1999
Review: Karen Owen

Cambria — Midsummer 2000

The Independent — 27 July 2000

The Week — 7 April 2001
Review: Andrew Lambirth

Western Mail — 13 July 2002
Review: Karen Price

Golwg — 8 Awst 2002
Review: Rhian Price

Planet, The Welsh Internationalist — No 154 Aug/Sept 2002
Review: Alistair Crawford

The New Welsh Review — No 59 Spring 2003
Review: Shelagh Hourahane

The Times — 3 December 2003
Review: John Russell Taylor

Western Mail — 6 Feb 2006

Galleries — February 2004
Review: Sarah Drury

David Jones Journal — Winter 2004/Spring 2005
Review: Robert A Newell

The Spectator — 22 January 2005
Review: Andrew Lambirth of 'Critic's Choice' exhibition

The Times — 2 February 2005
Review: John Russell Taylor

The London Magazine — February/March 2005

David Jones Journal — Winter 2004/Spring 2005
Review: Robert A Newell

Western Mail — 30 Sept 2005
Review: Kate Lloyd

The Spectator — 18 November 2006
Review: Andrew Lambirth

Western Mail — 19 October 2007
Review: Jenny White

Galleries — May 2008
Review: Blake Hall

The Artist — June 2008
Review: Oliver Lange

Financial Times — May 17/18 2008
Article: Simon de Burton

Antiques Magazine — May 23 2008
Review: Phil Ellis

Planet, The Welsh Internationalist — June/July 2008
Review: David Moore

The Week — 28 June 2008

The Spectator — 26 July 2008
Review: Andrew Lambirth

The Art Book — August 2008
Review: Julian Freeman

Country Life — January 7 2009
Review: Catherine Milner of 'Modern Art in Wales' exhibition. Pallant House

The Spectator — 31 January 2009
Review: Andrew Lambirth

Financial Times — January 31/February 1 2009
Review Jackie Wullschlager

Galleries — February 2009
(Front cover)

Western Mail — 17 October 2009
Review Jenny White

Western Mail — 26 October 2009
Review Darryl Corner

The Big Issue — 30 November 2009

The Spectator — 11 December 2010
Review Andrew Lambirth

The Times — 9 June 2012
Review John Russell Taylor

Western Mail — 8 February 2013
Review Jenny White

Wall Street International — 5 September 2013
Web article

The Spectator — 21 September 2013
Article by Andrew Lambirth

Prospect — 24 September 2013
Article by David Killen

Platform 505.com — September 2013
Web article by Susan Heywood

PUBLICATIONS AND ARTICLES

Exhibition catalogue
Boundary Gallery, London
Introduction: Andrew Lambirth 1995

Exhibition catalogue
'Ysbrydoliaeth. R S Thomas. Inspiration'
Oriel Plas Glyn-y-Weddw, Llanbedrog, Gwynedd 1995

Exhibition catalogue
West Wales Arts Centre, Fishguard
Introductions: Frances Spalding and Jill Piercy 1997

Arts Review
'Artist's Eye' April 1999

Royal Mail 1999 Year Book
'Royal Mail Millennium Stamps' 1999

Exhibition catalogue
West Wales Arts Centre, Fishguard
Introduction: Nicholas Usherwood 2000

David Jones Journal
'A Diary Remembered, June 1998' Summer 2000

Monograph
'David Tress' by Clare Rendell
Introduction: John Russell Taylor
Published: Gomer Press, Llandysul, and West Wales Arts Centre, Fishguard 2002

Exhibition catalogue
Museum of Modern Art Wales
Introduction: Dr Peter Wakelin 2003

Exhibition catalogue
'David Tress. Drawings'. Travelling exhibition
Published: West Wales Arts Centre, Fishguard
Text Andrew Lambirth 2003

The Jackdaw
'Easel Words' September 2006

Galleries Magazine
'Nuts and Bolts' about the 'Chasing Sublime Light' exhibition. Sarah Drury October 2007

Exhibition catalogue
'A Passion for Art'. The Friends of the Glynn Vivian Art Gallery 50th Anniversary Exhibition 2008

Exhibition catalogue
'Chasing Sublime Light'.
Introduction by Ian Jeffrey 2008

Artists and Illustrators magazine.
Articles by Jenny White April & Dec. 2008

Country Life
'New Romantic' about the 'Chasing Sublime Light' exhibition.
Mary Miers May 21 2008

Tivyside Advertiser
Article by Sarah-Jane Jones June 3 2008

www.resurgence.org web article
'Truth to Experience'
by Jeremy Hooker Jan/Feb 2009

Golwg
'Stiwdio'r Artist' Rhagfyr 10 2009

Exhibition catalogue
'The Rude and Beautiful Landscape'.
John Davies Gallery, Moreton-in-Marsh.
Introduction John Russell Taylor. 2009

Exhibition catalogue
'Landmarks'. Victoria Art Gallery, Bath.
Introduction Jon Bennington. 2010

Exhibition catalogue
'Earth, sun, wind & rain'. John Davies Gallery, Moreton-in-Marsh. Introduction – interview with David Tress by John Davies. 2011

Exhibition catalogue
'David Tress. In Search of the Sublime'.
Messum's Fine Art, London. Introduction by Andrew Lambirth 2012

Exhibition catalogue
'David Tress. A group of eleven new works'.
John Davies Gallery, Moreton-in-Marsh.
Introduction – interview with David Tress by John Davies. 2012

Exhibition catalogue.
'David Tress'. Messum's Fine Art, London.
Introduction by John Russell Taylor. 2013

Exhibition catalogue.
'David Tress. The Freshness of the Day'.
John Davies Gallery, Moreton-in-Marsh.
Introduction – interview with David Tress by John Davies. 2014

Exhibition catalogue.
'David Tress'. Messum's Fine Art, London.
Introduction by Andrew Lambirth. 2015

Monograph
'David Tress' by Andrew Lambirth
Published: Studio publications 2015

SELECTED TELEVISION AND RADIO

HTV Film
'Three Landscape Painters' 7 November 1994

BBC Choice
'Wrap' 7 September 1999

HTV Film
'River Patrol', featuring artists in Wales 21 August 2000

BBC Radio Wales
'First Hand' 9 July 2002

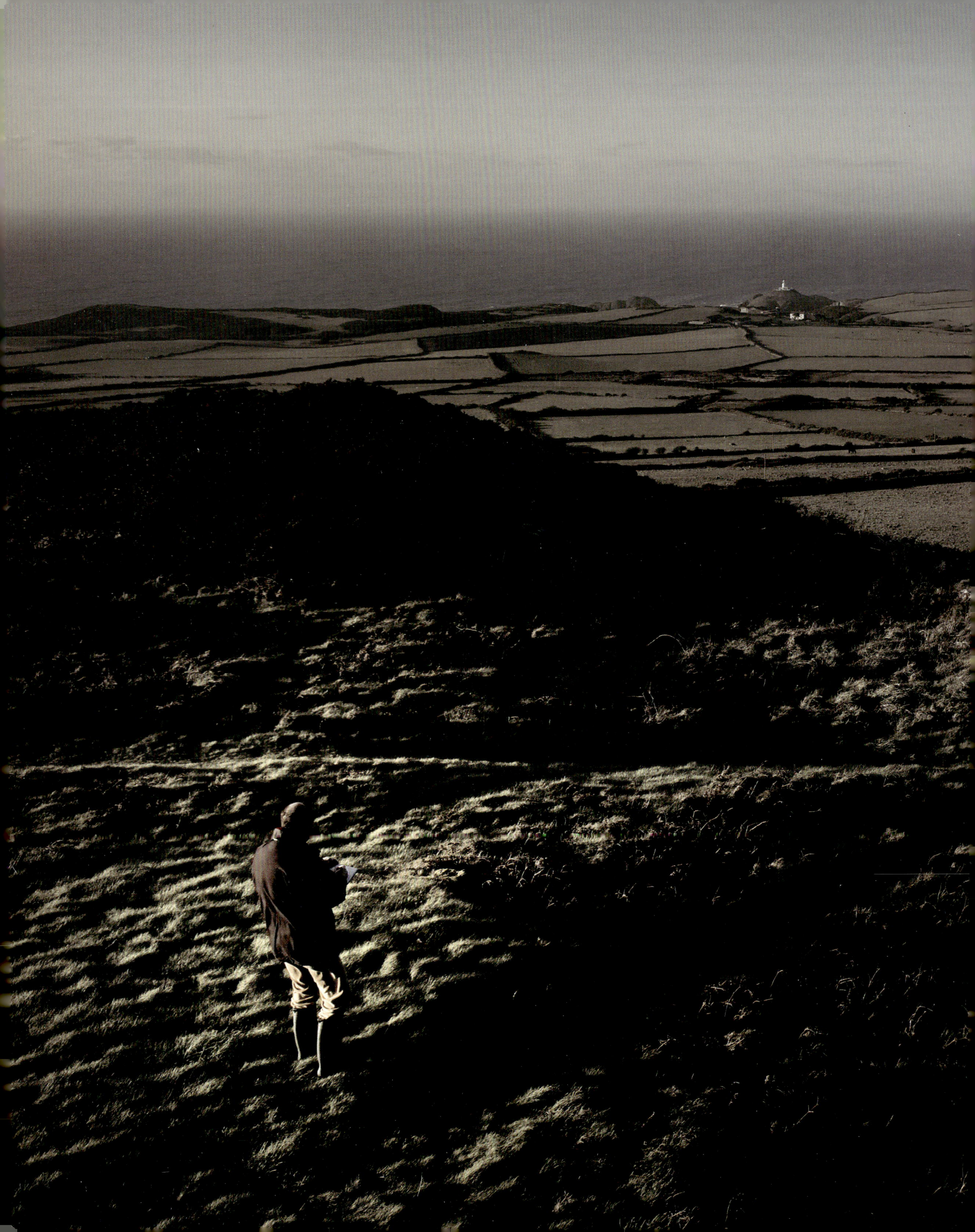